The Price Guide to
POT-LIDS
and other Underglaze Multicolour Prints on Ware

2nd Edition

by A. Ball

Antique Collectors' Club Ltd.

© 1980
A. Ball

World copyright reserved

ISBN 0 902028 56 1

British Library CIP Data
Ball, Abraham
     Price Guide to Pot Lids and other underglaze
     multicolour prints on ware.
     1. Pottery — Collectors and collecting
     2. Transfer-printing
     3. Glazing (Ceramics)
     I. Title   II. Antique Collectors' Club
     738.3′7   NK4230

         Published for the Antique Collectors' Club
           by the Antique Collectors' Club Ltd.

*Frontispiece: A selection of pots and lids which have extra
embellishments and colourings. These attractive items are very
rare, due, no doubt, to the extra work and expense involved in
producing them.*

Printed in England by
Baron Publishing, Woodbridge, Suffolk

Dedication

To my wife
the most dedicated collector of all
Also to all collectors of pot-lids
past, present and future

Acknowledgements

To all the friends and fellow collectors who have given freely of their time and knowledge in helping to compile this book, and in particular to Elizabeth Watson for her much appreciated assistance with the proofs. To Frank Cooper for his usual excellent photography, and last but not least, to Hilda for her patience in typing the whole of the manuscript.

Why not join —

The Antique Collectors' Club

The Antique Collectors' Club was formed in 1966 and now has a five figure membership spread throughout the world. It publishes the only independently run monthly antiques magazine *Antique Collecting* which caters for those collectors who are interested in increasing their knowledge of antiques, both by increasing the members' knowledge of quality and discussing the factors which influence the price that is likely to be asked. The Antique Collectors' Club pioneered the provision of information on prices for collectors and still leads in the provision of detailed articles on a variety of subjects.

It was in response to the enormous demand for information on "what to pay" that the price guide series was introduced in 1968 with the first edition of *The Price Guide to Antique Furniture,* a book which broke new ground by illustrating the more common types of antique furniture, the sort that collectors could buy in shops and at auctions, rather than the rare museum pieces which had previously been used (and still to a large extent are used) to make up the limited amount of illustrations in books published by commercial publishers. Many other price guides have followed, all copiously illustrated, and greatly appreciated by collectors for the valuable information they contain, quite apart from prices.

Club membership, which is open to all collectors, costs £7.95 per annum. Members receive free of charge *Antique Collecting,* the Club's magazine (published every month except August), which contains well-illustrated articles dealing with the practical aspects of collecting not normally dealt with by magazines. Prices, features of value, investment potential, fakes and forgeries are all given prominence in the magazine.

Among other facilities available through the Club are private buying and selling facilities, the longest list of "For Sales" of any antiques magazine, an annual ceramics conference and the opportunity to meet other collectors at your local antique collectors' club. There are nearly eighty in Britain and so far a dozen overseas.

As its motto implies, the Club is an amateur organisation designed to help collectors to get the most out of their hobby: it is informal and friendly and gives enormous enjoyment to all concerned.

For Collectors — By Collectors — About Collecting

The Antique Collectors' Club, 5 Church Street, Woodbridge, Suffolk

Contents

Introduction 9

Bear Subjects 17

Pegwell Bay Subjects 26

Potted Meat and Fish Paste Jars 51

Personal Adornment Subjects 66

Floral Subjects 78

Exhibition Subjects 89

Portrait Subjects 97

Historic Buildings 113

War and Geographical Subjects 125

Shakespearian Subjects 134

Old English Scenes 137

Sports and Pastimes 145

Dogs and other Animals 158

Birds 171

Pictorial, Landscape and General Subjects 184

Ware and Trinket Set Accessories 228

Additional Items 284

Glossary 287

Appendix I   Copper Plates at Coalport 295

Appendix II   Book of Factory Pulls 304

Appendix III   Wares produced by Mayers 307

Appendix IV   Pot-Lids based on Contemporary Paintings and Prints 308

Appendix V   Historical Notes 313

Index 315

Preface

Over the past fifty years there have been numerous articles and writings on the subject of 'pot-lids', or, to give the correct title, 'underglaze multicolour printing on ceramic wares'.

There have also been several books written during this period, all of which are to be commended, but there has been a notable omission, namely colour printing on articles other than pot-lids, for instance, dessert ware, cups and saucers, jugs, toilet ware and other similar items. This book is designed to overcome this omission by giving the reader as complete a picture as is possible of all known items which have been decorated by the process of underglaze multicolour printing.

The reason for this omission in the past was due to certain factors:

1. 'Pot-lids', as a generic name, is an ordinary term which everyone is capable of understanding, not only because it describes their purpose, but also gives a reference for collecting. This meant that preference was given to the term 'pot-lids' as against the expression 'underglaze multicolour printing on pottery'.
2. 'Pot-lids' preceded the wares (with the exceptions mentioned in the book).
3. Pot-lids do not require as much room for display.
4. Pot-lids were the preference of earlier collectors, and this preference has persisted up to the present time.
5. Pot-lids were easier to come by, owing to the very large quantities produced.
6. Possibly more lids have been saved relative to the ware. The lid, once it had been used, would either be discarded or saved, whereas the wares would be used each day over and over again, thereby giving more opportunities for breakages. This had the effect of making ware rarer and therefore a less 'popular' subject for writers. This situation is now understood and it is hoped this book will do much to rectify the anomaly.

The purpose therefore, of this book is to show not only pot-lids but also the comparable items which are complementary to them, whilst at the same time attempting to give an approximate idea of values.

Whilst I hope that this book is the most comprehensive yet written on underglaze multicolour printing (Prattware and pot-lids), it is realised that to include and describe every known piece of underglaze multicolour printing is a task which would daunt even the most optimistic. This preface admits such omissions and apologises for them.

It is felt that a good general description will help all collectors, if it can also be remembered that certain items do have extra embellishments (exhibition subjects for example) which may not have been mentioned in this Guide; in such cases prices must be adjusted accordingly.

Due to the inevitable delay between the preparation of the manuscript and the printing of this book, the prices of some items may have changed. These will be adjusted with publication of the annual price revision list.

A. Ball, December 1979

Introduction

To understand and appreciate more fully the items one collects, it is necessary to acquire as much knowledge as possible relative to one's interest. Therefore, it is imperative that the development of the art of colour printing be traced from its initial inception to the present time. Very briefly, then, these notes are written to help in this understanding.

Colour printing was first introduced in the middle of the fifteenth century, when special parts of books, such as initial letters, were printed using wood blocks which had been carved with the design required. The principle used was similar to the one used today, that is, covering the surface of the block with colour and then placing the page over the block and applying pressure. This method is called relief printing. Many efforts were made over the years to improve the process, but it was not until late in the eighteenth century, when the first iron press was invented, that any appreciable advance was recognised.

This next method was called *intaglio* printing and consisted of using copper or steel plates which were engraved by different means, such as stipple, line or mezzotint; in fact, the reverse of relief printing.

Thus we arrive at the most common method of all, lithography, which was discovered by Aloysius Senefelder towards the end of the 18th century. This method consisted of using large flat stones, with the picture to be printed drawn directly on to a stone; it was found that transfers could be taken directly from the stone. If several stones were used showing the same print or drawing, and by using different colours on each stone, a colour picture could be produced.

Lithography was in its heyday from the early nineteenth century until the early twentieth century. Contemporary with this art, was the method used by George Baxter, who took out a patent in 1835 for a process which combined most of the systems previously mentioned with the addition of special oils mixed with his colours. The process was registered as 'Baxter's Patent Oil Printing'.

It must be remembered that up to this period, all efforts towards colour printing had been directed at printing on paper. This, obviously, was a situation which had to change, and there are records available which show that, circa 1847, a previous apprentice of George Baxter, one A. Reynolds, took a position with the noted ceramic firm of Mintons, Stoke-on-Trent, who at that time were experimenting with colour printed tiles. It is more than coincidence, surely, that the first colour printed wares made their appearance at this time and that the method being used followed so closely the ideas of George Baxter.

The concise history of early colour printing below is followed by a more detailed account up to the period where it was adopted by the ceramic firms of Pratt, Mayer, Cauldon etc.

1486   Earliest example of colour printing in the *Book of St. Albans*. Wood blocks for relief printing.

1720   J. Le Blon (not to be confused with the later nineteenth century colour printer Le Blond), invented the method of engraving copper or steel plates, and by using three plates, each with one of the positive colours of red, blue and yellow, was able to produce a printed colour picture.

| 1760 | The art of printing in one colour (monochrome), on ceramic wares was discovered, reputedly by Sadler and Green of Liverpool, who solved the problem by adapting the system of engraving copper and steel plates, by using transfers from the copper plates on the ware. |

| c.1800 | It was discovered that lithography could be adapted for use on ceramic wares. |

| 1835 | George Baxter invented his colour printing process by using a combination of the two methods previously mentioned, i.e. relief and *intaglio*. He would first engrave the picture he intended to produce on a steel plate. This plate would then be inked with the outline colour and impressions taken, using a press. Blocks would be cut to suit the colours required and impressions would be taken. |

It should be noted that Baxter varied this arrangement and also used steel plates for his various colours. The advantage Baxter had over his predecessors was his ability to break down a picture into its component colours, some of his prints requiring twenty or more blocks to produce the end effect. The disadvantages of his process were that reproductions could only be produced on paper and were expensive to produce, whilst lithographic prints were not only cheaper to print, but could also be used on ceramic wares, although the quality was inferior to Baxter's patent printing method.

| 1845-47 | Colour printing on ceramic wares has become a reality. By combining a number of the foregoing methods, a process evolved whereby colour printing could be used on items other than paper. The factories concerned were few in number, producing items suitable for this type of colour printed decoration. To ensure a viable commercial proposition, it was necessary for these wares to be produced in very large quantities and important, therefore, that a common cheap type of pottery earthenware was used and that the factories concerned should be in the immediate locality. |

The tragedy is that the advantages of the process have in fact proved to be its disadvantages. The system as adapted for use on ware, as well as the results obtained, were better than anything seen before (as today's collectors well know), but because the uses to which the wares were put were so utilitarian, recognition was not given to the process or its products at the time of manufacture. The wares were accepted as pleasant objects ancillary to other table wares. There seems little doubt that an element of Victorian snobbery was responsible for preventing the ware from taking its rightful place in history, alongside Worcester, Derby and Spode. For this reason this book concentrates on the period from approximately 1845, when multicolour printed wares were first introduced, until the 1900s.

We have seen that monochrome transfer printed wares had been in vogue since approximately 1760. By the early nineteenth century most factories were using this method of decoration not only for high class wares but also for utilitarian wares of every description, not the least of which were pots and boxes used as containers for ointments, greases, pastes, etc., whose lids were transfer printed either with a pictorial design or suitable wording to show the contents. These boxes and lids were made mainly in the Potteries and since the experiments in multicolour underglaze printing were taking place there, what was more natural than to use the prints on the local pottery?

One of the firms which supplied large numbers of monochrome pots and lids to manufacturers throughout the world was F. and R. Pratt and Co., of High Street, Fenton,

Stoke-on-Trent. This firm was noted for its excellent productions in this field, chiefly due to the efforts of the proprietor Felix Edwards Pratt (1813-1894) and his very talented chief engraver Jesse Austin (1806-1879). The method used by Austin was very much akin to the one used by George Baxter, the main difference being that Baxter's outline printing came first, whilst Austin's was applied last.

At this stage it is appropriate to explain the application in colour printing in more detail:—

1. A drawing of the subject was made.[1]
2. From the drawing copper plates were engraved, dissecting the colours into their constituent parts. This was done by no more than three or four plates. If a fourth plate was found necessary, it was always green or damson. Then the outline plate of either brown or black completed the process. The sequence of plates is given below:

    > Buff or yellow
    > Blue
    > Red or pink
    > Green or damson
    > Black or brown

3. Each plate would be 'charged' with the colour to be used. The colour was mixed with a preparation of hot oil and the engraved portion of the plate filled with colour, using a flat palette knife for the purpose. The surplus would be scraped off and replaced in the receptacle containing the oil and colour mixture.
4. Next, a sheet of special tissue paper was laid over the plate and pressure applied by passing both plate and paper through rollers on a machine very similar to the old-fashioned mangle.
5. The paper at this stage would retain the impression from the plate and would then be passed from the printer to the transferrer, who would lay it over the lid or item to be decorated. The lid at this point, still being in its biscuit state, that is, fired but unglazed. The transferrer would then apply pressure, either with a strong bristled brush or a roll of flannel-like material called a 'boss' and, when he considered the impression had been transferred, the surplus paper was washed away.
6. The lid would then be taken to a 'drying shed' for approximately two days, until the colour was absorbed and the oil had dried out.
7. The whole process would then start again (as described from paragraph three), and be repeated again and again for each colour, making sure, by means of the small dots seen on each side of the print, that each colour was in register.
8. After the last colour had been transferred and dried out, the lids were then dipped in liquid glaze and again fired at a lower temperature than previously. On completion of this firing, the glaze was fused to the lid, the colours being revealed for the first time since the whole operation started.
9. If gold decoration was required, another firing was necessary at a lower temperature to fix the gold over the glaze.

The usual pattern apparently, was to produce more than one print at a time — two is the most common number per plate, but there are exceptions, varying from one to four. So that

Footnote
1. Early research into the origin of the prints used in underglaze multicolour printing attributed them in the main to drawings by Jesse Austin, who was employed by Messrs. F. and R. Pratt, and by Bates, Brown, Westhead-Moore and Co. but later findings show that these prints were mainly copied from contemporary paintings. Appendix IV gives a list of the subjects of pot-lids linked to known contemporary prints.

the process can be clearly understood, there is a colour illustration showing a lid at varying stages of production on page 15. The lids would normally only be glazed and fired after the final colour had been transferred.

A recent examination of the copper plates now in the possession of Coalport revealed that the plates were previously in the possession of Cauldon Potteries and are the combined copper engraving plates of both Messrs. F. and R. Pratt and Cauldon Potteries Ltd. Pratts had run into financial difficulties in the early 1920s and had sold all their assets to Cauldon, including the Jesse Austin engraved copper plates. Examination of these copper plates show that some have a Cauldon mark

Royal Cauldon
England
Est. 1774

engraved in addition to the print. It is reasonable to assume that all such plates have been reissued at some time and this mark used as a back stamp for reference, although copper plates without this back stamp may also have been reissued.

Some of these plates also have an engraved number and, after much checking, it appears that the plates so numbered are from the Pratt factory. This again does not mean that all others which are not numbered are from some other factory, but the gap is considerably narrowed when we check the lists as shown against the full known list of pot-lid pictures. Appendix I (page 295) gives the complete list of known pot-lids, showing the numbers assigned to the Coalport copper plates by H.G. Clarke in 1924, and revised numbers (as used throughout this book) made necessary by the later discoveries of prints made by factories other than Pratts.

As may be seen from the chart below, the fortunes of the Pratt and Cauldon companies became inextricably combined in later years and it is therefore difficult to decide who actually manufactured some of the prints. Appendix II shows details of the book of factory pulls kept for reference at the Cauldon/Pratt factory.

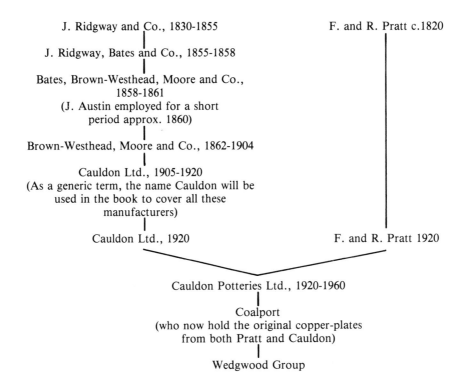

J. Ridgway and Co., 1830-1855
|
J. Ridgway, Bates and Co., 1855-1858
|
Bates, Brown-Westhead, Moore and Co.,
1858-1861
(J. Austin employed for a short
period approx. 1860)
|
Brown-Westhead, Moore and Co., 1862-1904
|
Cauldon Ltd., 1905-1920
(As a generic term, the name Cauldon will be
used in the book to cover all these
manufacturers)
|
Cauldon Ltd., 1920

F. and R. Pratt c.1820

F. and R. Pratt 1920

Cauldon Potteries Ltd., 1920-1960
|
Coalport
(who now hold the original copper-plates
from both Pratt and Cauldon)
|
Wedgwood Group

Records of the Mayer factory are not as well documented as those of Cauldon and Pratt, but the following is a list of the changes in the ownership of the factory up to the present.

T.J. and J. Mayer	1843-1855	
Mayer Bros. and Elliott	1855-1858	
Mayer and Elliott	1858-1861	
Liddle, Elliott and Co.	1861-1870	
Bates, Elliott and Co.	1870-1875	Possibly the same Bates that joined J. Ridgway in 1855
Bates, Walker and Co.	1875-1878	and left that company in 1861, just about the time J.
Bates, Gildea and Walker	1878-1881	Austin joined J. Ridgway.
J. Gildea, Walker and Co.	1881-1885	
J. Gildea	1885-1888	
Keeling and Co.	1888	
Kirkhams	1890	Copper plates acquired and lids were reissued from this date until the factory was taken under the control of Portmeirion Potteries in 1962.
Portmeirion Potteries	1962	

Obviously, these three firms of Pratt, Cauldon and Mayer produced the greater volume of underglazed colour printed wares, and certainly most of the reissues were produced by these same firms. The following points may assist the reader in distinguishing between originals and reissues.

1. Originals are lids or ware which were produced up to approximately 1900, and were actually used for their original purpose.

2. Originals can be referred to as 'very early', 'early' or 'late', as distinct from 'reissues'.
   (a) 'very early'   — 1845-1860 ⎞
   (b) 'early'   — 1860-1875 ⎬ approximately
   (c) 'late'   — 1875-1900 ⎠
   (d) 'reissues' — 1900-present (produced solely for decorative purposes and never used as lids).

3. Several distinguishing features are taken into account when deciding the category.
   (a) **'very early'**
       Flat top -- very often black border — small crazing — usually seen as Bear or Pegwell Bay subjects — good colours.
   (b) **'early'**
       Convex top — small crazing — good colours. Note: both (a) and (b) very often have details shown of either contents or the customer's name.
   (c) **'late'**
       Heavier in texture — usually poorer colours — larger and more uniform crazing — details omitted as on earlier lids, such as registration marks and names, which again are referred to later.
   (d) **'reissues' — from Kirkhams[1]**
       Usually flat tops — no crazing — two holes in top rim for hanging purposes, which show glazing (not to be confused with original lids which have been drilled for the same purpose and are unglazed on the inside of the drilled holes) — very heavy in texture — may be inscribed on the underside with 'Coloured prints from the Original Plates Engraved for the Jesse Austin Process, 1845-1870', or 'Reproduced by Kirkhams Ltd., Stoke-on-Trent, England. 1947'. Note: collectors should beware of lids with inscriptions which have been obliterated either by being painted over on the reverse or by being filled with plaster.

Footnote
1. Appendix III lists the wares produced by the Mayer factory and items known to have been reissued by Kirkhams.

'reissues' — from Cauldon

Ware of a lighter and creamier texture, becoming more of a porcellaneous body — usually larger crazing — often poor colours — dessert plates may carry an embossed border and are generally without crazing, but colours are mainly good, very often printed marks, e.g. "This picture is printed from the Original Engravings used for the Old English Pot-Lids made by Messrs. F. and R. Pratt of Fenton, about 1850 to 1860" or "The Pictures on these pots are printed from the Original Engravings used for the Old English Pot-Lids now so valued by Collectors, and made by Messrs. F. and R. Pratt of Fenton about 1850-1860".

'reissues' — from Coalport

Very light in texture — small rim — china body — good colours but hard in appearance. Inscription on reverse "This rare Pot-Lid is reprinted from the Original Pratt Engraving and is one of a limited edition made specially for Clarkson of Wolverhampton by Coalport China, owners of the engravings for these prints."

In 1975 the Wedgwood group began reissuing the following limited editions of ware using the old copper-plates, under the Coalport label:

Series 1 (Pot-Lids)
The Waterfall
St. Paul's and River Pageant
Bear Hunting
The Dentist
The Maidservant
The Swing

Series 2 (Bird Plates)
Pair of Wrens
Thrushes
Robin
Blue Tit and Long-tailed Tit
Snowy Owl and Young
Reed Warblers

Series 3 (Miscellany)
Pair of vases with dog prints
Pair of dishes (Llangollen)
(Two Anglers)
Pot-Lids (Village Wakes)
(Parish Beadle)
(Christmas Eve)

Series 4 (Bird Plates)
The Heron
Eagle Owl and Merlin

Although the factory of origin of most pot-lids is now established, there remain a few whose manufacturers are still unknown; these are given below.

No.	Title	No.	Title
7*	Bears Reading Newspaper	130*	The Bee-hive
8	The Attacking Bears	171*	Peabody
11*	Bear with Valentines	184	The Houses of Parliament
12*	The Performing Bear	186	Tower of London (Entered at
14*	Bear in a Ravine		Stationers Hall)
17	Arctic Expedition in search of	189	Westminster Abbey (Entered at
	Sir John Franklin		Stationers Hall)
18	Polar Bears	192	St. Paul's Cathedral (Entered at
33	Pegwell Bay (Shrimping)		Stationers Hall)
59*	Fisherwomen Returning Home	195	New Houses of Parliament (Entered
61*	River Scene with Boat (R.W.)		at Stationers Hall)
65*	Swiss Riverside Scene	268*	A Gay Dog
107*	Lady with Guitar	320*	Mother and Daughters
124*	Bay of Naples	355*	Royal Coat of Arms
125**	Gothic Archway	367	How I Love to Laugh
129*	Royal Arms and Allied Flags of the	438	Unwelcome Attentions
	Crimea		

* *Probably produced by Pratt/Cauldon.*
** *Possibly Mayers.*

A lid at the various stages of production. (a) A lid in its biscuit state with yellow only applied. (b) The same lid glazed and fired. (c) A lid with yellow and blue applied in its biscuit state. (d) The same lid glazed and fired. (e) A lid with yellow, blue and red applied in its biscuit state. (f) The same lid glazed and fired. (g) A lid with the three colours yellow, blue and red plus the outline applied in its biscuit state. (h) The same lid glazed and fired, showing the completed process.

Other factories which have produced underglaze multicolour prints, on a much smaller scale, and definitely of an inferior quality, include:

Wm. Smith and Co., Stockton-on-Tees
Livesley, Powell and Co., Hanley, Stoke-on-Trent
G.L. Ashworth and Bros., Hanley, Stoke-on-Trent   Only seen on ware
Morgan, Wood and Co., Burslem, Stoke-on-Trent
Wood and Baggaley, Burslem, Stoke-on-Trent

It is hoped that these remarks concerning the methods of production, styling, dating, naming of reissues, details of factories etc., will help all collectors to increase and improve their knowledge of underglaze multicolour printing on ceramic wares.

Price Revision List

February annually
(The first list will be published in 1981)

The usefulness of a book containing prices rapidly diminishes as market values change, for prices can fall as well as rise.

In order to keep the prices in this book fully up-dated, a revised price list will be issued in February each year. This list will contain the current values of all the pieces illustrated in the book.

To ensure that you receive the Price Revision List yearly, complete a banker's order form and send it to the Antique Collectors' Club now.

The Price Revision List costs £1.87 a year by banker's order or £1.95 cash, from:—

THE ANTIQUE COLLECTORS' CLUB
5 CHURCH STREET, WOODBRIDGE
SUFFOLK

Bear Subjects

No. 1 Alas! Poor Bruin

There are two versions of this print, one has a lantern on the end of the inn sign, the other has no lantern. The title is at the foot within the print. A print produced by the Pratt factory c.1850 but has been reissued many times since that date, and the copper plates used for this print are still in existence (see list of copper plates, Appendix I). Used also on items of ware such as tobacco jars and plates. Of particular interest, this is one of the prints included on a set of small plates, 5½ins. diameter, with blue surround.

(a)	Print to edge of lid.	£30—£50
(b)	Print with double line border.	£20—£30
(c)	Print with extra fancy border in brown.	£30—£50
(d)	Print with extra white surround.	£20—£30

Tobacco Jars £100+   Plates £25—£40

No. 2 Bear Attacked by Dogs

There are several varieties of this lid. Another print from the Pratt factory c.1850 which was adapted by Jesse Austin from a painting by 'Snyders'. No reissues are known and the copper plates appear to be lost; they are not included in the list shown earlier. Unrecorded on ware.

(a)	Printed to edge of lid........	£100—£150
(b)	Double line border..........	£80—£120
(c)	White surround............	£80—£120
(d)	Gold line, white surround....	£120—£150
(e)	Gold band ¼ in. wide........	£150—£200

No. 3 Bear's Grease Manufacturer

A very rare print which has never been seen on ware and only one copy of this lid has been found, produced by Mayer Bros., c.1850. A double line border encircles the print with the wording 'Clayton & Co's Real Bear's Grease, 58, Watling St, London' round the rim. No reissues of this lid have ever been seen.

P.B.N.

No. 4 Bear Hunting

Unrecorded on ware, from the Pratt factory, c.1845-60. Will be found in three sizes: (a) the smaller size has the print with the wording 'Ross & Sons' Genuine Bear's Grease perfumed. 119 & 120, Bishopgate Street, London' round the outside edge; (b) the medium size is similar, with the addition of a black and blue chequered border plus an outer gold line; (c) the large size has a further geometrical style border and was a later production. The address is shown as 120, Bishopgate Street only. Earlier editions have the address as 119, Bishopgate Street only. Copper plates still in existence (see Appendix I). Produced on china by Coalport in 1973 in a limited edition.

(a)	*Without border but with lettering*	*£80—£150*
(b)	*With border chequered*	*£100—£175*
(c)	*Large size with extra borders*	*£100—£175*

No. 5 The Prowling Bear

Not seen on any items of ware. This is a very scarce lid and is similar to Lid No. 122, 'Meditation', in as much that they both have the wording 'Robt. Smith & Co. London' round the outer rim. This lid cannot, with certainty, be ascribed to any particular factory, it does not appear in any records available, but was probably manufactured by T.J. & J. Mayer, who produced the companion lid, 'Meditation'. The date of production was approximately mid-1840 and no reissues have ever been seen.

£300 — £500

No. 6 The Bear Pit

Unrecorded on ware, this pot-lid was produced originally at the Pratt factory c.1850, with many reissues at later dates. There are a considerable number of variations of this lid, the main one being with or without a dome over the ostrich's cage. The copper plates are still in existence, which show the dome over the cage and also a fancy border; obviously, these plates were altered, probably due to excessive wear. There can be no doubt whatever on the origin of this print, Jesse Austin's drawing is still in existence and the plates are definitely Pratt/Cauldon as previously mentioned.

(a)	*With dome*..............................	*£30—£50*
(b)	*With extra fancy border*...................	*£40—£60*
(c)	*Without dome*..........................	*£30—£50*
(d)	*Without dome with fancy border*...........	*£40—£60*

No. 7 Bears Reading Newspapers

Unrecorded on ware. Possibly produced by J. Ridgway c.1850. Credit for this lid has been attributed to F. & R. Pratt and also to T.J. & J. Mayer by previous writers but, surely when this lid is compared with No. 12 'The Performing Bear', and the two varieties of No. 208 'Sebastopol', which were produced by J. Ridgway, the similarity is too obvious to be ignored. No reissues have been seen of this print. Print usually to edge of lid; if a larger size was required, a white surround was added.

£300 — £500

No. 8 The Attacking Bears

Unrecorded on ware, a very early lid, possibly c.1850, and does not appear to have been produced at the factories of either Pratt, Mayer or Ridgway. Not as colourful as the usual multicolour prints but a very great rarity.

P.B.N.

No. 9 Bears at School

Unrecorded on ware, an early lid from the Pratt factory. Several alterations were made on this plate, mainly to the foliage. It has either double line border or line and dot border. No reissues of this lid have been seen and the copper plates are not included in Appendix I.

£35 — £50

No. 10 Bears on Rock

Only found on lids. Produced by the factory of T.J. & J. Mayer, possibly about 1850. No reissues have been seen. Will be found in two sizes, small and medium, and in varying colours of either black or red-brown bears. The larger size has been seen with the number 6 stamped on the reverse; this usually is confirmation of the factory of origin. Not a very well produced lid.

Small   £35—£50
Medium   £35—£50

No. 11 Bear with Valentines

Unrecorded on ware, this, again, is one of the early lids which are extremely difficult to relate to any one particular factory. There are no records available which mention or show this print, and the colouring and texture are completely different from the usual ones seen. The comparison with lids from the factories of Pratt, Mayers, Cauldon, etc., show these differences. Probably produced by J. Ridgway & Co., who only made small quantities, which could be one of the reasons for the extreme scarcity of this lid.

£300 — £500

No. 12 The Performing Bear

A very early lid produced by an unidentified factory but could possibly be J. Ridgway, owing to the similarity to the lids 'Bears reading Newspaper', No. 7, and both varieties of 'Sebastopol', No. 208. Unrecorded on ware, this lid and also the others mentioned are rather poor in colouring, and the production, particularly as it affects the registration, seem to lack the quality seen in later prints. One of the extremely rare lids.

£250 — £350

No. 13 Shooting Bears

A Pratt lid which has been reissued many times since the original lids were issued, c.1850. This print is also in the Pratt factory sample book (Appendix II). Unrecorded on ware. There are a number of variations to be seen — with bushes to the right of the man loading the gun — without the bushes — the bears are shown as either reddish-brown or black, but the most obvious changes are in the sizes: (a) the smallest size is printed to the edge of lid; (b) the medium size has the wording 'Ross & Sons Genuine Bears Grease Perfumed' with the address either 119 Bishopgate Street or 119 & 120 Bishopgate Street, London round the rim; (c) without the wording, but with a white surround. The print is copied from a painting entitled 'Bear Hunt in the Pyrenees', seen in the *Illustrated London News*, dated 29th January 1853.

> (a) £40—£60
> (b) £75—£100
> (c) £40—£60

No. 14 Bear in a Ravine

An early print which is as yet unidentified in origin but could be Ridgways, the firm who produced lids for Whitaker's (see Nos. 124 and 127 for details). A particularly pleasant lid of excellent production and shows stippling similar to Pratts. Wording round the print reads 'Whitaker & Co's Genuine Bears Grease. 69 Hatton Garden, London'. The print shows a bear facing towards the left and the whole is in delicate shades of black, green, pink and blue with a double black line border edged with gold. A very scarce lid and again no ware has been seen bearing this print.

P.B.N.

No. 15 The Ins

No. 16 The Outs

As is usual with these early lids, no ware has been seen with either of these prints. Presumed to have been produced at the Pratt factory but this cannot be taken for granted, as no definite proof is available. The only information available is that H.G. Clarke included these two lids in his original list as produced at Pratts but the copper plates for these prints are not included in the list from Pratts (Appendix I). The appearance of these two lids lead one to assume that they were made at the Cauldon factory when in the possession of J. Ridgway, about 1850.

> *Double line border*   £80—£120
> *Fancy border*   £100—£120

No. 17 Arctic Expedition in search of Sir John Franklin

Unrecorded on ware, another early lid from an unidentified factory. In previous writings, credit has been given to both Mayers and Ridgways for this lid, but no proof exists. A Baxter print (shown above right) bearing the same title was published in 1850 and there is little doubt that this lid was adapted from the print as published. This scene has always been supposed to represent an incident in an expedition led by Sir John Ross to search for Sir John Franklin. Courtney Lewis, in his book on George Baxter, makes this statement and it has since been repeated by other writers, but in fact the incident depicted happened to the expedition which sailed in 1848 in the ships *Enterprise* and *Investigator,* and the actual incident took place about May 1849. This particular expedition was led by the nephew of Sir John Ross, who did not lead *his* expedition until 1850.

> *Either variety*
> *Double line border*   £120—£180
> *Single line border*   £120—£180

No. 18 Polar Bears

One of the earliest colour printed lids whose manufacture is still a matter of supposition. H.G. Clarke, in his earlier writings, states that Mr. E. Etheridge was shown an entry in the ledger of a chemist in Blackfriars, which substantiated the statement that these lids were purchased by the owner in 1846 but, unfortunately, the name of the vendor was not recorded. Apart from the sections in white, this lid is printed only in two colours, green and blue. As is usual with early lids, this print is not seen on ware of any description.

Without moon	*£80—£120*
With moon	*£100—£150*

No. 19 Bear, Lion and Cock

Produced by the Pratt factory possibly about 1854-55, this is confirmed by the political allusion shown, with Russia the seated bear, apparently being threatened by Britain represented by the lion, and France as the cockerel, overseeing the proceedings. The copper plates for this lid are still in existence and lids have been produced at various times over the years. Will be found with or without the title at the foot and sometimes with the addition of a white surround. The later lids are seen with an extra fancy border and the steeple of St. Martin's Church is deleted from the print.

Line and dot border	*£40—£60*
White surround	*£40—£60*
Fancy border	*£50—£75*

No. 20 All but Trapped

Produced by the Mayer factory about the same period as the preceding lid, 'Bear, Lion and Cock', with its obvious allusion to the Crimean war of 1854-56. No ware seen with this print. Certain of these lids show the potter's number on the reverse; such numbers are only seen on Mayer lids.

Line border	*£150—£250*
Fancy border	*£200—£300*

No. 21 Bear in Cave

Very similar to lid No. 14, factory unknown, the bear in this instance is facing in the opposite direction and is encircled by a floral border. Two copies only of this lid have been seen, one complete with mottled surround and base.

P.B.N.

Pegwell Bay Subjects

Queen Victoria, before her accession to the throne in 1837, visited Ramsgate in 1830 with her mother, the Duchess of Kent, where, no doubt, she tried the potted shrimps produced at the nearby Pegwell Bay fishing village.

On her accession a Royal Warrant was issued to Tatnell & Son as 'Purveyors of essence of shrimps and potted shrimps in ordinary to Her Majesty'.

No. 23 Pegwell Bay

A very early and extremely scarce lid from an unidentified factory, but could possibly be a Mayer production. Very early lids usually have a flat top and this lid is no exception; later examples of lids have a slightly domed top. The blue colour rather predominates, and this lid could possibly be one of the first, about 1848, before the method of underglaze colour printing was actually successful. Usually printed to the edge of the lid with wavy line border, but later editions have a white surround. The name 'Pegwell Bay' is printed in capitals on both types. Not seen on any other kind of ware.

P.B.N.

No. 24 Pegwell Bay (Lobster Fishing)

A very colourful and well made Mayer lid, produced in the 1850s. The medium lid has double line border and is also printed to the edge of the lid. The larger size has a fleur-de-lys border with broad gold line, very similar in design to the two jars numbered 67 and 68. Both lids have the title 'Pegwell Bay' at the foot, but later issues can be seen without the title. The wording Tatnell & Son is often seen on the house in the foreground.

Medium size	£40—£50
Large size with fleur-de-lys border	£50—£75

No. 25 Pegwell Bay. Established 1760

Two varieties of this lid are known: the earlier edition shows a sandy pathway, whilst the later edition has a grassy pathway. Produced by the Pratt factory c.1860-65 and unrecorded on ware.

Either variety £25 — £40

No. 26 Pegwell Bay — Four Shrimpers

No definite proof of factory of origin, but certain details point to the Cauldon factory when in the ownership of either John Ridgway or T.C. Brown, Westhead, Moore & Co. One very strong reason is that the name 'S. Banger' is occasionally seen on the underside of this lid and this is the manufacturer's name used on the pots or lids containing fish pastes etc., produced by him at Pegwell Bay in the mid-19th century. It is assumed that lids bearing this name 'S. Banger' were produced at Cauldon, whereas lids bearing a similar manufacturer's name, i.e. 'Tatnell & Son', were produced by Mayers. Another reason is that both the shapes and the prints are not quite as well produced as either Pratts or Mayers, the registration and colouring not being quite up to standard. Two varieties are known, both with and without the title 'Pegwell Bay' seen at the foot, within the double line border. The earlier variety has the title. Unrecorded on ware.

Either variety £25 — £40

No. 27 Belle Vue Tavern (with cart)

Rather heavy and flattish in shape, one of the very early lids, c.1850. Presumed to have been manufactured at the Mayer factory, although there is now some doubt. A drawing of this subject by J. Austin exists but he never worked for T.J. & J. Mayer. A scarce lid with an advertising reference to 'Tatnell & Son' which can be seen on the cart and also on the building.

£200 — £300

No. 28 Bell Vue Tavern (with carriage)

A later and more attractive lid than the previous one, No. 27. A similar scene except that a carriage replaces the cart and possibly produced for the same fish-paste manufacturers by F. & R. Pratt. This supposition is borne out by the fact that the copper plates are still in existence as shown in Appendix I. This lid is also shown in the Pratt factory book of pulls (Appendix II). Unrecorded on ware.

£25 — £40

No. 29 Belle Vue Tavern

This lid creates a doubt as to the factory of manufacture, but comparisons and examinations show that there are two different varieties. The first, or earlier lid, was most probably made by T.J. & J. Mayer; this is a rather flat top lid which may have the wording 'Tatnell' either on the underside or on the building in the foreground, or no name showing at all, the cliffs in this case being a dark colour. The second, or later lid, appears to have been produced at the Cauldon factory when owned either by John Ridgway or T.C. Brown, Westhead, Moore & Co. In this instance the cliffs shown are white, and the name 'S. Banger' is seen either on the building or on the underside. There is also a white border around the wavy line border seen on both varieties. Neither variety is seen on ware.

With dark cliffs   £60—£80
With white cliffs   £50—£75

No. 30 Belle Vue — Pegwell Bay

Again, there are two varieties of this lid: the earlier and usually more colourful one has no bay on the lower window shown on the building, and possibly this lid was manufactured at the Mayer factory. The later one was definitely produced by F. & R. Pratt (see the list of copper plates in Appendix I), showing a bay window, and has been seen in the Pratt factory book of pulls (Appendix II). The title is shown at the foot on both lids. Unrecorded on ware.

Without bay windows   *£30—£50*
With bay windows   *£25—£40*

No. 31 Pegwell Bay Shrimpers

A lid which has been attributed to both F. & R. Pratt and the Mayer factory, but no definite proof exists of which factory produced this unusual lid. Apart from minor variations such as number of vessels, two main versions were produced. In one a sailing vessel can be seen apparently jutting out of the cliffs on the right. The two jars Nos. 67 and 68 show this same scene and also this same anomaly. It appears that the transfer referred to above, i.e. the sailing vesssel projecting from the cliff, was cut and used for this scene. This is verified by comparing the two prints, and the deleted sections are then most noticeable. The name 'Banger' seen on the building to the left leads one to assume that F. & R. Pratt were the manufacturers, but the very poor quality of the colour and registration must leave a doubt, especially when it is observed that this print is not included in the list of surviving copper plates from Pratts, and is not shown in the factory book of pulls. Not seen on other items than lids and jars.

With sailing vessel in cliffs   *£80—£120*
Other varieties   *£25—£40*

29

No. 32 Pegwell Bay
S. Banger, Shrimp Sauce Manufacturer

Again, no definite proof of manufacture, the copper plates are not included in the list (Appendix I), and this print is not shown in the Pratt factory book of pulls (Appendix II). It will be seen that the name of S. Banger is displayed no less than three times on the print. Obviously this makes it very doubtful that Mayers produced this lid (their lids usually advertised Tatnells), and points to the Cauldon factory when owned by either J. Ridgway or T.C. Brown, Westhead, Moore & Co. A lid very similar to both Nos. 27 and 28, but shows the shop of S. Banger in place of the Belle Vue Tavern. Two sizes were produced: the larger size has the title 'Pegwell Bay' at the foot, outside a double line border, the smaller size having the same title at the foot of the print within a decorative border, and also the wording 'S. Banger, Pegwell Bay, Nr. Ramsgate' within an oval on the reverse. Only seen on lids.

Large size   £125—£200
Medium size   £100—£150

No. 33 Pegwell Bay (Shrimping)

A print which is only seen on lids and is still to be identified as to the factory of origin. Two varieties of this lid are known; the earlier and better produced one has a flat top, deeper colours, and is printed to the edge of the lid with a single line border. The later variety has a domed top and is much thicker and heavier in texture, with a white surround to the edge of the lid. On both varieties the word 'Shrimping' is seen within a scroll at the top of the lid, and the title 'Pegwell Bay' also within a scroll, at the foot. Possibly one of the earlier lids from about 1850.

Flat top   £50-£75
Domed top   £40—£60

No. 34 The Dutch Fisherman

Most likely from the Mayer factory, c.1850, but it is difficult to understand why so few of these particular lids are still in existence. The usual situation is that the very scarce lids, such as this one, are produced by minor unidentified factories, but there is very strong evidence to support the view that this is definitely a 'Mayer' lid. Two varieties are known; one variety has the wording 'Tatnell & Son' at the top with 'Pegwell Bay' at the foot. The other variety has no wording. As with other early prints, this subject does not appear on any other kind of ware. The subject of this print appears to have been very freely adapted from a painting by H. Gastineau, entitled Shakespeare's Cliff, Dover, which was published in 1828 in the *Picturesque Beauties of Great Britain* (see below).

Either variety £300 — £500

**No. 35 Pegwell Bay, Ramsgate
(Still-life Game)**

**No. 36 Pegwell Bay, Ramsgate
(Still-life Fish)**

These three lids constitute a series which were produced by T.J. & J. Mayer in the 1850s and were produced over a period of many years. This series is not seen on ware. All three lids were issued either with print to the edge of the lid, with a double line border or with an extra gold line. Lids can have the wording 'Tatnell & Sons, Pegwell Bay, Ramsgate' at the foot, or are unnamed. 'The Farmyard Scene' No. 37 was adapted from a painting by T.S. Cooper entitled 'The Farmyard' (see below right). No. 36 'Still-life Fish' has been seen in an extra large size with the wording 'Potted Bloaters' or 'Potted Anchovies' surrounding the picture.

Nos. 35	*Print to edge of lid*	*£40—£60*	*No. 36*	*Double line border*	*£60—£80*
and 37	*Double line border*	*£40—£60*		*Gold line*	*£75—£100*
	Gold line	*£50—£75*		*Print to edge of lid*	*£60—£80*
	Extra large	*£50—£75*		*Extra large*	*£75—£100*

**No. 37 Pegwell Bay, Ramsgate
(Farmyard Scene)**

A selection of jugs in various styles and colourings. Occasionally, jugs are seen as a personal item, for instance the middle jug on the second row from the top carried the name and date — William Gallimore 1868 — in gilt script.

No. 38 Landing the Fare — Pegwell Bay

An early lid produced at the Cauldon factory by either J. Ridgway, Bates & Co., or Bates, Brown-Westhead, Moore & Co., c.1850-60. No reissues of this lid have been seen, and it is not included in either the list of existing copper plates or the factory book of pulls, both of which relate to the Cauldon/Pratt factories. Some of the lids may have the name of 'Banger' on the underside. Unrecorded on ware.

£30—£50

No. 39 New Jetty and Pier, Margate

As with No. 38, this lid and also the following lids, Nos. 40, 41, 42 and 43, were probably produced by the Cauldon factory during the period c.1850-60. The title is at the foot and the whole is enclosed within a double line border, also produced without the title. An extra large size lid, which again is not seen on ware of any kind. The subject of this print was taken from a painting, possibly by W.H. Bartlett, which was published in 1835 in the *Watering Places of Great Britain and Fashionable Directory*.

£30 — £50

No. 40 The Harbour, Margate

A lid which was produced in two sizes, medium and large, the details as for Nos. 38 and 39. No doubt this print was copied from a contemporary drawing or painting of the period but, as yet, has not been identified. The title is at the foot of both sizes of lid and again, unrecorded on ware.

Medium £20—£30
Large £25—£40

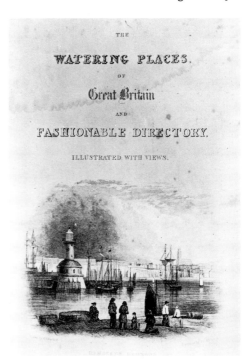

No. 41 Royal Harbour, Ramsgate

A large lid with a fancy border of triangular design, with particulars as quoted for lids Nos. 38, 39 and 40. This particular print was probably copied from the frontispiece to the *Watering Places of Great Britain and Fashionable Directory* (see illustration) published in 1835. Not used on any kind of ware and the title is shown at the foot within the print.

£25 — £40

No. 42 Royal Harbour, Ramsgate

A companion lid to No. 41, which shows the view from the sea, whilst this one, No. 42, shows the view looking out to sea. All details are as for pot-lids Nos. 38-41. Again not seen on ware, this lid was produced in two sizes — medium and large — with either flat top or slightly domed, the title as above, within the print at the foot.

Medium   £20—£30
Large   £25—£40

No. 43 Nelson Crescent, Ramsgate

An extra large lid produced at the Cauldon factory (details as for lids 38-42). Only the one size is known, but there are differences in the colouring, and one set of plates apparently gives a much deeper reddish colour. The title is within the print at the foot, the whole enclosed by a double line border.

£40 — £60

No. 44 Sandown Castle, Kent

An early lid produced at the Mayer factory, c.1850. Only produced in the one size, medium. Title is seen at the foot and lids will be found with the wording 'Tatnell & Son' on the underside. This lid is interesting in as much that it remains as a memorial to a castle which was demolished in 1864 owing to the inroads of the sea. Unrecorded on ware.

£75 — £100

No. 45 Walmer Castle

A lid not seen in either the list of existing copper plates or factory book of pulls, yet all the evidence points to this lid being produced at the Cauldon factory whilst owned by either J. Ridgway & Co., or Bates, Brown-Westhead, Moore & Co. The evidence becomes irrefutable when, on re-checking previous research by other writers, it is noted that these missing copper plates and records always show prints which are never recorded on any other item than lids. If this statement is checked back on other items quoted in this book, it will be seen to be correct, leaving one to make the assumption that, prior to Jesse Austin's period of employment at Cauldon (c.1860), no records or copper places were preserved, which also means that no late issues or reissues were ever produced.

£25 — £40

No. 47 Walmer Castle

This lid was noted by G.H. Gibson in 1934 as appearing in the list of transfers which showed the various prints produced by T.J. & J. Mayer. Perhaps this is correct, but there is one slight anomaly; on the underside of some of these lids are the words 'Banger — Pegwell Bay'. Previous research shows Cauldon/Pratt lids being used by this firm 'Banger', with 'Tatnell' lids being produced by 'Mayers'. However, in view of the fact that G.H. Gibson's list is so well authenticated, it is most likely to be a 'Mayers' lid. One size only, with double line border. Unrecorded on ware.

£80 — £120

No. 46 Walmer Castle (with sentry)

Produced at the factory of T.J. & J. Mayer, with the wording 'Tatnell & Son, Manufacturers, Pegwell Bay, Nr. Ramsgate', enclosed within an oval design, on the underside of some of the lids. This very scarce lid is on record as showing the favourite residence of the famous Duke of Wellington. One size only, and again, not seen on ware of any description. The title is shown at the foot within the double line border.

£100 — £150

No. 48 Pretty Kettle of Fish

There are three different issues of this lid, which was first produced at the Pratt factory, possibly about 1850-60. The first issue has square window panes and the title at the foot within the print, the whole surrounded by a scroll border. The second issue also has square window panes but no title. The third issue has diamond shaped window panes, also no title, but has the addition of a red cloth over a wooden seat. This print was apparently used on lids over many years, but is not seen on other types of ware. This lid and No. 49, 'Lobster Sauce', form a pair.

1st issue	*£50—£75*
2nd issue	*£30—£50*
3rd issue	*£20—£30*

No. 49 Lobster Sauce

As with No. 48, 'Pretty Kettle of Fish', this lid was produced at Pratts factory contemporary with that lid. Again, three issues were produced: the first issue with the title at the foot and no window showing; the second issue was very similar but the title was omitted; the third issue has windows showing with red curtains and no title. Produced over many years as a pair with No. 48. Both lids Nos. 48 and 49 are shown in the factory book of pulls and the copper plates are still in existence.

1st issue	*£50—£75*
2nd issue	*£30—£50*
3rd issue	*£20—£30*
Tea plates	*£20—£30*

No. 50 Injury

These two lids form a pair and were manufactured by Bates, Elliott & Co., who registered these prints on June 11th 1873 and are marked accordingly on the underside. The diamond registration mark was used between 1842 and 1883. Then the system of registration was changed to a method of numbering and after 1883 no registration was necessary and no markings are seen. Both lids are only in the one size.

With registration   £50—£80
Without registration   £30—£50

No. 51 Revenge

No. 52 Shells

There are a number of different designs bearing shells, and these are shown on the following pages, numbered 52A—52L. They were used on various items of ware, and several factories were responsible for the production. T.J. & J. Mayer and their successors, and F. & R. Pratt were the main manufacturers, but examples have been seen from other factories. Either 'Cockson & Harding' or 'Charles Hobson' could have produced shell wares, as jugs and plates have been seen with the initials C.H. on a garter shaped scroll, the pattern name 'Shells' contained within the scroll. There are quite large numbers of items still available bearing shells as their main theme, such as jugs, mugs, plates, door furniture, cups and saucers, etc., and it is noted that valuations can vary considerably, according to the ground-laid colour, shape, rarity or condition, especially if the water jugs still retain their metal cover. It should be noted that, although these designs are popular, the copper plates are not mentioned in the existing list of such plates, neither are they included in the factory book of pulls (Appendix I and II), which leads one to suppose that no reissues of the known and illustrated subjects were ever produced. The period of manufacture was approximately 1860-1890. Items from the Mayer factory with these prints have been seen marked July 1862, Jan. 1863, April 1865 and June 1870.

Jugs	*£20—£30*
Mugs	*£15—£30*
Tea-pots	*£30—£40*
Tea-pot stands	*£10—£20*
Cups and saucers	*£25—£35*
Mustard pots	*£25—£35*
Plates	*£10—£20*
Soap dishes	*£30—£40*
Door furniture	*£20—£30*

Shell subjects 52A, 52B, 52D, 52J and 52K are also seen on lids, with 52A being the rarest.

52A	*lid*	*£50—£75*
52B	*lid*	*£25—£40*
52D	*lid*	*£25—£40*
52J	*lid*	*£25—£40*
52K	*lid*	*£25—£40*

Two new shell items have now been recorded:—
1. Puzzle jug with Shells No. 52H
2. Cheese dish with Shells No. 52G

52A

52A

52B

52B

52C

52C

52C

52D

52D

52D

52F

When this you see
Remember me
For I am your friend
That makes good tea.

A PRESENT
From
BLACKPOOL

52G

52G

52G

52 I

52J

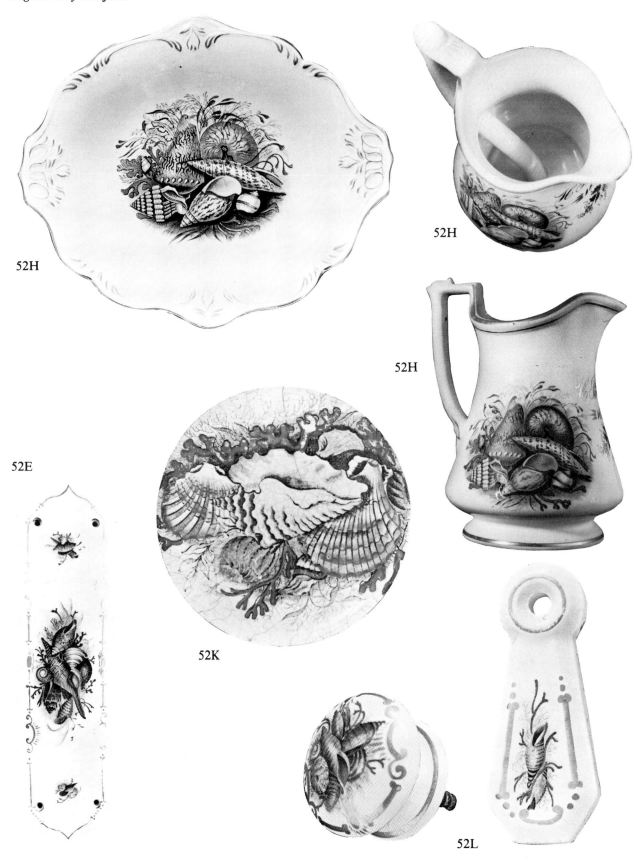

52H

52H

52H

52E

52K

52L

No. 53 Hauling in the Trawl

A very common lid produced by the Pratt factory over a period of many years. First manufactured c.1860, for the firm of Crosse & Blackwell, according to a label which has been seen affixed to the underside of a particular lid with this print (see illustration). Not seen on ware, but this does not rule out the possibility, as from this period it is noticeable that dessert services and plates with underglaze colour prints were becoming very popular. Reissues could have been produced, as this print is listed both in the list of copper plates and also the factory book of pulls (Appendix I and II). Copied from a painting, 'Herring Fishing, Isle-of-Man', shown as a drawing in *The Illustrated London News,* 6th March 1847.

£20 — £30

No. 54 Examining the Nets

Again a very popular lid from the Pratt factory. Usually only seen in the one size, with a pearl dot border, but it may be seen from the factory sample book and from the existing list of copper plates that this print was also used on ware, without the border. This is one of the few prints (when used on ware) to carry an extra colour — green.

Lids	*£25—£40*
Plates	*£15—£25*

No. 55 Landing the Catch

There is plenty of evidence to suggest this was produced by F. & R. Pratt. Not only is this print included in the list of copper plates and also in the book of pulls (Appendix I and II), but the watercolour by Jesse Austin is still in existence. Printed either with double line border or to edge of lid. Also seen on ware.

Lids	£25—£40
Tea plates	£15—£25

No. 56 Mending the Nets

An early lid from the Mayer factory. Attribution has previously been given to F. & R. Pratt for this lid, but recently lids have been seen with markings on the underside which are usually only seen on 'Mayer' lids. In this example the number 3 is on the underside. One size only with double line border and extra white surround. Not seen on ware of any kind.

£25 — £40

No. 57 The Fishmarket

A lid from the Mayer factory very similar in style and colouring to No. 56. The number 3 is found on the underside on certain lids. Several varieties are known — double line border, also with extra gold line, and printed to edge of lid. Unrecorded on ware.

All varieties £25 — £40

No. 58 The Fishbarrow

An early 'Pratt' lid which was in production for many years. Several varieties are known, some have a lace design border, some have an additional raised decorative border outside the inner lace design border, and some lids have Jesse Austin's signature. The drawing by J. Austin is still in existence, but it is not original. It was copied from a painting by Jan Steen. May also be seen on ware, particularly on the three-sided vases seen with the portrait of Alexis Soyer, the chef employed by Crosse & Blackwell, and also on other more decorative triangular shaped vases with either No. 311, 'I see you, my boy', No. 348, 'Peasant Boys', or No. 349, 'The poultry-woman'.

Raised border lid	£25—£40	Green and maroon	P.B.N.
Lace design border	£25—£40	Gold and yellow	P.B.N.
	Soyer vase £250 plus		

No. 59 Fisherwomen Returning Home

One of the few lids for which the factory of origin cannot be identified at present. Two different issues of this lid are known; the earlier one is printed to edge of lid and has a flat top, and the later one has a domed top and a gold line round the print. There is a certain similarity between this lid and Nos. 61 and 65, which are also unauthenticated, but there is also a very strong affinity with Nos. 60-62 and 66, which are shown in the Pratt factory book of pulls. One can assume, therefore, that all these lids were possibly produced by the Cauldon/Pratt concerns in the 1850s. As is usual with most early lids, these prints are not seen on ware.

Flat top	*£50—£80*
Domed top	*£35—£50*

No. 61 River Scene with Boat (R.W.)

No certain proof as to the factory, but more than likely to have been manufactured by F. & R. Pratt, c.1850. This lid was produced in two sizes, medium and small, both sizes have a twisted rope border. In the foreground is a boat with the letters R.W. painted on each side of the rudder.

Either size £80 — £120

No. 60 The Net-mender

An early lid manufactured by Pratts, this print is included in the factory book of pulls (Appendix II), but is missing from the list of existing copper plates. It will be noticed that the lids Nos. 59, 60, 61, 62, 65 and 66 all have more green incorporated in the print than the usual colours seen. This is more evidence that all the lids mentioned may have been produced at the same factory c.1850. Only seen on lids, which is usual for prints as produced in this early period. Medium size only with flat top and gold line border. Later issues have domed top.

Flat top	*£50—£80*
Domed top	*£35—£50*

No. 62 Foreign River Scene
A Pratt lid which is shown in the factory book of pulls (Appendix II), but is not in the list of existing copper plates. A large lid, produced in one size only, the print being encircled with a gold line border, c.1850. Not seen on ware.

£60 — £80

No. 63 The Shrimpers
A very popular lid made by F. & R. Pratt c.1850, but has been reissued many times since that date. Several different varieties were produced, which show how often the copper plates were re-conditioned. Some of the lids are signed with the initials J.A. and others show three huts replacing a chapel. The print in the factory book shows two boats to the left of the picture, but no houses, this obviously being the latest issue. The original watercolour drawing by Jesse Austin is still in existence, but again it was not original. In this instance it was copied from two paintings, both by W. Collins, R.A., the 'Prawn Fishers' and also 'The Young Shrimpers' (see illustrations).

£20 — £30

No. 64 Sea Nymph with Trident

There are two quite different varieties of this lid which was produced by F. & R. Pratt and Cauldon. It is possible that the Cauldon factory may have produced the earlier lid from J. Austin's drawing (still in existence), followed by the later edition from the Pratt factory. The earlier lid is of much better quality, showing stronger and deeper colours, with a purple cloak, whereas the later issue is much heavier in texture, the cloak is blue and the lid also has a rather flat top. Not seen on ware.

> *Blue cloak*   £80—£120
> *Purple cloak*   £100—£150

No. 65 Swiss Riverside Scene

As with No. 59, 'Fisherwomen returning home', it is very difficult to find actual proof of where this lid was produced; also with the lids previously mentioned in this group, i.e. 59, 60, 61, 62 and 66, all are very well produced, with the difference in colouring (green) showing up very strongly.

> *£50 — £75*

No. 66 Dutch River Scene

Evidence points to this lid being produced by either Cauldon or Pratt; as will be seen, this lid together with Nos. 60 and 62 are included in the factory book of pulls, but are not in the list of surviving copper plates. It is difficult to understand why Nos. 60, 62 and 66 are included, and not Nos. 59, 61 and 65, which are so similar in production.

> *£50 — £75*

Potted Meat and Fish Paste Jars

No. 67 Pegwell Bay and Cliffs

Two fish-paste jars, assumed to be from the Pratt factory possibly in the early 1850s. The anomaly here is that the ship apparently sails into the cliff. This is due to the foreshortening of the transfer which appears as a duplication on each side of jar No. 68, whereas jar No. 67 is a complete print encircling the jar. A variation on lid No. 31, 'Pegwell Bay Shrimpers', which shows the same foreshortening effect.

No. 67 Without vessel in side of cliff   £25—£40
No. 68 With vessel in side of cliff   £80—£120

No. 68 Pegwell Bay and Cliffs (sailing vessel in the side of the cliff)

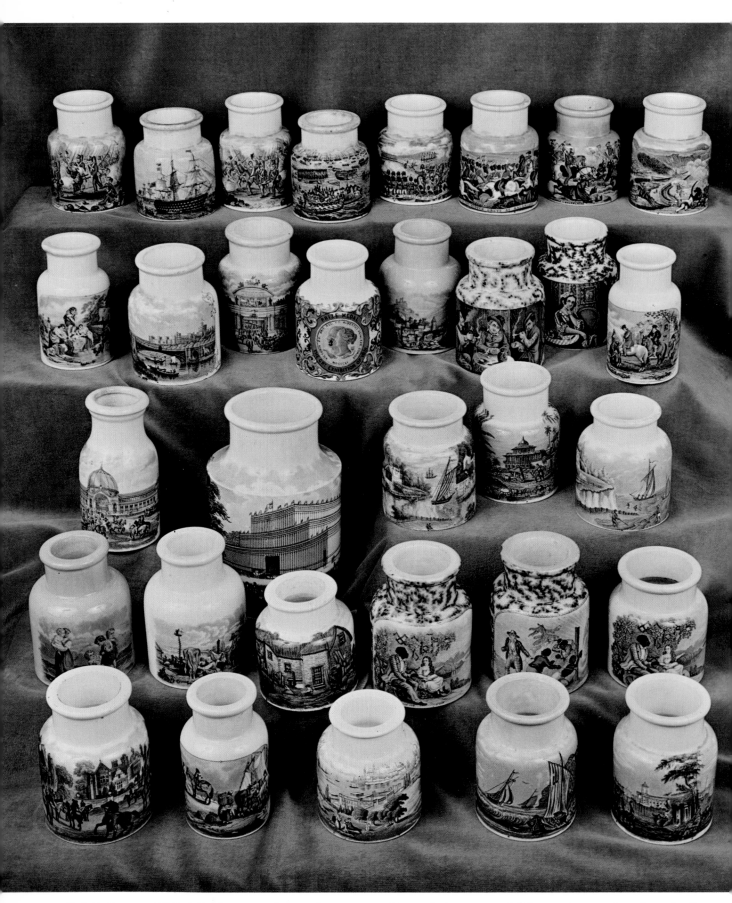

F. & R. Pratt and T.J. & J. Mayer were the two firms concerned in producing meat and fish paste jars , such as these, for the processing trade. Of particular interest are the jars on the top row, produced by T.J. & J. Mayer and relating to the Crimean War. Note the extremely rare jar, in the middle of the third row, on which can be seen a sailing vessel, apparently sailing into the cliff.

No. 69 Pegwell Bay — Kent

From the Mayer factory, usually found with
the distinctive Mayer numbering on the base.
The title is seen in the body of the print.
£20 — £40

No. 70 Mending the Nets

Both jars, Nos. 70 and 71, are presumed to have
been made at the factory of F. & R. Pratt. There is
definite evidence with regard to No. 71 as it is
included in the factory book of pulls, and also in
the list of existing copper plates (Appendix I and
II). No. 70 is apparently taken from the same
source as the Le Blond oval, 'The Fisherman's
hut' (see illustration). No titles are shown.

No. 70   £30—£40
No. 71   £20—£30

No. 71 Continental Fish Market

Nos. 72-79 Crimean War Jars

The next eight jars all emanate from the Mayer factory and depict scenes from the Crimean war, and therefore they could possibly have been produced during the period of T.J. & J. Mayer. All these jars have the distinguishing Mayer numbering, usually either a 6 or a 7. Nos. 78 and 79 are identical except for the title. See Appendix V for the historical background to Nos. 74-77.

No. 72	*The Fleet at anchor*	*£150—£200*
No. 73	*Landing of the British army at the Crimea*	*£125—£175*
No. 74	*Battle of the Alma (20th Sept. 1854)*	*£75—£100*
No. 75	*Battle of the Alma*	*£75—£100*
No. 76	*Charge of the Scots Greys at Balaklava*	*£60—£80*
No. 77	*The Dragoon charge — Balaklava*	*£60—£80*
No. 78	*The fall of Sebastopol (8th Sept. 1855)*	*£60—£80*
No. 79	*Sir Harry Jones*	*£60—£80*

No. 72 The Fleet at Anchor

No. 73 Landing of the British Army at the Crimea

**No. 74 Battle of the Alma
(20th Sept. 1854)**

No. 75 Battle of the Alma

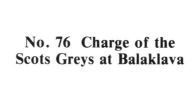

**No. 76 Charge of the
Scots Greys at Balaklava**

**No. 77
The Dragoon Charge —
Balaklava**

**No. 78 The Fall of Sebastopol
(8th Sept. 1855)**

No. 79 Sir Harry Jones

No. 80 Constantinople — The Golden Horn

This print is identical to No. 204 'The Golden Horn, Constantinople', and both are possibly the products of the Cauldon factory during the period of J. Ridgway & Co., which would date them c.1850-55.

£25 — £40

81 Meet of the Foxhounds

A very fine jar produced by F. & R. Pratt. This print is listed in the factory book of pulls and the copper plates are still in existence (Appendix I and II).

£25 — £40

No. 82 The Traveller's Departure

From the Pratt factory, included in both the list of copper plates and the factory book of pulls (Appendix I and II). This print was produced, not only on a jar, but also on an oblong lid and various items of ware. All these items are shown with the same title, but are listed under number 396. The watercolour drawing by J. Austin is still in existence, but this again is not original in design. It was copied from a painting by Cuyp, the Dutch painter.

£50 — £80

57

No. 83 The Chalees Satoon

This is a very finely printed jar from the Mayer factory. The print, which is repeated (to encircle the jar), depicts a pavilion, which is attached to the Emperor's Palace at Allahabad, at a spot where the Ganges and Jumna unite. A Baxter print (see illustration) bearing the same title and showing the same scene, was published in 1848, followed by a further edition in 1850. This means, of course, that it is extremely difficult to decide which came first, the jar or the print, especially when it is realised that the scene as shown, was copied from a painting by W. Daniell, R.A.

£50 — £80

No. 84 Venice

Again from the Mayer factory and this jar will quite often be seen with the very distinctive Mayer number printed on the base, in this instance, No. 3. The print is repeated, as with No. 83, 'Chalees Satoon', so that the jar is encircled, but, just as the previous print was a copy of the Baxter print, so this one is an exact copy of the Le Blond print of the same title, which was used as an illustration for a pocket book in 1851 (see illustration). The view shows on the left the 'Church of Sta Maria della Salute' and the entrance to the Grand Canal. St. Marks is on the right in the distance. Two issues of this jar are known; one shows the man on the steps facing the gondola, the other shows him with his back to the gondola.

Either variety £30 — £50

No. 85 Alexandra Palace — 1873

Produced at the factory of F. & R. Pratt, obviously, rather later in period than most of the jars already listed, possibly about 1874. This particular print served a dual purpose: not only was it used on a jar, it was also used on the rectangular lid and base with the same title (see No. 200). These later jars are always elongated in appearance, whereas the earlier ones are of a more squat design. A further point to note is that whereas the Mayer jars usually carry a title, the Pratt ones do not have this distinction.

£25 — £40

No. 86 Milking the Cow

Another dual purpose print produced by F. & R. Pratt. Not only was this print used for this jar, it was also used on a rectangular lid of the same name, No. 391. As is usual with the jars produced by this firm, no name is shown, but the title was adopted by J. Austin when he produced the watercolour drawing, which is still in existence. This drawing was copied from a painting entitled 'The Studio of Paul Potter' and was painted by Le Poittevin, a celebrated French painter of the seventeenth century (see illustration). There is no doubt about the authenticity of this print. In addition to the watercolour, the copper plates still exist and it is also illustrated in the factory book of pulls (Appendix I and II).

£75 — £100

No. 87 Tyrolese Village Scene

Obviously a similar pattern here, as with the Pratt jars previously mentioned. This print served a dual purpose by being used on the rectangular lid, No. 397, with the same title. The jar is much rarer than the lids. This is also true of other cases in which a print was used on both jars and lids. The watercolour by J. Austin is still in existence, but again, it is not original. The painting from which it was copied is titled 'St. Goar on the Rhine'.

£40 — £75

No. 88 The Torrent

Although this print was used for other purposes, it has not been seen on a lid. With the same title, but with the number 411, as in this book, it was used on articles of dessert ware, loving cups, mugs, tobacco jars, cups and saucers, etc. From the Pratt factory, this is one of the few subjects which were printed in five colours, the extra colour being green in this instance. The copper plates are still in existence, and it is also shown in the factory book of pulls (Appendix I and II).

£40 — £75

No. 89 The Stone Jetty

A very similar jar to No. 82, 'The Travellers Departure', and No. 88 'The Torrent'. Reference to the list of existing copper plates (Appendix I) will show that these three prints were all produced in one operation, due to the fact that all three are engraved on one plate. The green is again noticeable on this jar. The actual title of this painting is 'The Homeward Bound', painted by F.R. Lee, from which it was obviously copied by Jesse Austin when in the employ of F. & R. Pratt (see illustration). This same print was used many times on other items, on rectangular lids, either with or without trefoil ends, on cups, saucers, plates, etc. These are illustrated under No. 395.

£40 — £75

No. 90 Passing the Pipe

The same print as used on items of ware, see No. 404. Both this print, 'Passing the Pipe', and 'The Smokers' were engraved on one plate at the factory of F. & R. Pratt, and were probably first used about the mid-1850s on these jars, being used later for all the varied types of ware. Two sizes are known, one about 3¼ins. tall, the other variety about 3¾ins. tall, but, whilst the smaller size has a flat base, the taller one has a concave base, so that they both hold the same quantity of tobacco.

Either variety £60 — £80

No. 91 Uncle Tom and Eva

As is usual with so many of these prints which give details of contemporary events, no doubt F. & R. Pratt produced these particular ones to coincide with the visit of Harriett Beecher Stowe (see No. 172) to this country in 1853. See also Nos. 401 and 402 for the same prints used on oblong lids and also on ware. The two mottled jars each have one print only, 'Uncle Tom and Eva' as No. 401 and 'Uncle Tom' as No. 402, whereas the plain jar has both prints depicted. These copper plates are still preserved and are shown in the list compiled from the factory.

Uncle Tom (mottled)	*£75—£100*
Uncle Tom & Eva (mottled)	*£75—£100*
Both prints on white background	*£75—£100*
Set of three	*£250—£350*

No. 92 The Deer-Stalker   No. 92A Wild Deer

Adapted from two of Landseer's paintings 'On the look-out' and 'The Alarm', these prints are together on one copper plate and are still in existence, and an extra colour, green, was used for these prints. F. & R. Pratt registered the design on August 18th 1871 and the lids were produced later in the 1870s. These two prints were also used on lids of oblong shape with trefoil ends, see Nos. 384 and 385. It is unusual to find these jars with the covers as illustrated, and it is rather more unusual to find shaped pots. The more common ones have the straight sides.

Jar without lid	*£20—£30*
Jar with lid	*£20—£40*
Shaped jar without lid	*£30—£40*
Shaped jar with lid	*£40—£50*

No. 93 The Smokers

As with No. 90, 'Passing the Pipe', this is a print which was also used extensively on lids and ware, see No. 405. All details are as stated for No. 90, including the references to the different sizes.

Either variety £60 — £80

No. 94 St. Paul's Cathedral

A small barrel shaped jar produced by T.J. & J. Mayer, c.1850-1860, for the firm of Crosse & Blackwell. Occasionally these jars are found complete with a small shaped lid which fits inside the jar. The number 7 is sometimes printed on the base (not unusual for products of the Mayer factory).

£15 — £25

No. 95
Royal Exchange

A similar jar to No. 94, but much rarer. Obviously smaller quantities were produced for this firm of Stringer & Co.

£40 — £60

No. 95A Royal Coat of Arms

A similar jar to both Nos. 94 and 95, but it is printed in one colour only. This jar has printed on the base, 'Designed by Crosse & Blackwell May 1844'.

£15 — £25

No. 96 Reception of H.R.H. The Prince of Wales and Princess Alexandra at London Bridge
7th March 1863

Produced by F. & R. Pratt to commemorate the occasion of the marriage of H.R.H. Prince of Wales and Princess Alexandra. Two varieties of this jar are known — the earlier one being smaller in height but larger in diameter, and the later one being more elongated. The size of the earlier jar is 3¾ins. by 2¾ins., with the later one 4½ins. by 2½ins., and the scroll giving details of the occasion has been omitted from the later version. Reissues of this print were made on a mug in the 1960s.

Early variety   £60—£80
Later variety   £30—£50

No. 96A A Sea-shore Study

A very rare item from the Pratt factory, usually found on rectangular lids, see No. 393. The engraving for this print was copied by J. Austin from a book published in 1830 by Rogers, entitled 'Italy', which contained this painting by Stothard (see illustration).

£80 — £120

No. 96B Great Exhibition 1851

From the style and shape of this jar, it appears to have been produced at the factory of T.J. & J. Mayer in the early 1850s. Previously unrecorded, it shows the heads of Queen Victoria and Prince Albert within an elaborate scroll border, depicting a medal awarded to the firm of Copland & Co. for their products as displayed at the Exhibition of 1851. The reverse of the medal is also shown with a blank panel to allow for a description of the contents. The catalogue of the 1851 Exhibition describes this firm as producers of a new process in preserving fruits, jams, jellies, provisions etc., which can be hermetically sealed and retain their freshness for years.

£150 — £250

No. 96C Windsor Castle (Hill & Ledger)

Only recently illustrated, three examples of this very rare item have now been seen. The first recorded example of this jar was originally discovered in Bendigo, Australia, in 1955 during excavations being made whilst building was in progress. The building being demolished bore the date 1856, which substantiates the date of manufacture as possibly 1850-1860 by the factory of R.J. & J. Mayer for export to Australia. A further proof of manufacture is the usual Mayer number printed on the base, in this case it is 2.

£100 —- £200

No. 96D Exterior View, 1851 Exhibition

An extra large jar showing a panoramic view of the grounds and exterior view of the 1851 Exhibition in Hyde Park. This jar is much larger than any previously recorded, being 6ins. in height and 4ins. in diameter. Produced by the Mayer factory in the early 1850s, no doubt to commemorate the Exhibition. On the base is the usual Mayer numbering, in this case an 8. This jar is the only recorded example.

P.B.N.

Personal Adornment Subjects

No. 97 The Bride
Produced at the Mayer factory possibly early in the 1850s. There are two sizes, medium and small, with a variety of borders, such as line border only, line border with white surround or purple band and lace border.
Any variety £80 — £150

No. 98 An Eastern Repast
Very similar in style and contemporary with the previous lid, No. 97, and produced at the same factory. Two sizes are known, medium and small, with both sizes having a fancy chain design border.
Either size £50 — £80

No. 99 Eastern Lady Dressing Hair
Like Nos. 97 and 98, this lid was produced in two sizes, medium and small, by the Mayer factory in the 1850s. Both sizes have a fleur-de-lys border, the larger one with the addition of a number of black lines. There are a few minor differences in the two varieties. The woman in the smaller variety has darker hair and pearls over the left shoulder. Her dress is of a much lighter colour. There are fewer trees in the background. The name of 'Henry Trinder: London: 75 Watling Street, St. Pauls' will be seen on the underside of some of these lids.
Either variety £75 — £100

No. 100 Eastern Lady and Black Attendant

This very rare lid was produced in two sizes, small and medium by Ridgways at Cauldon, c.1830-1858. The medium lid has a blue band border added. Although it is very unusual to find early prints on ware, there is in existence a small decorative tazza displaying this print surrounded by crimson colouring and gold scroll-work.

Either small or medium lid   P.B.N.
Small decorative tazza   P.B.N.

No. 101 The Mirror

An early lid from the Pratt factory, issued in conjunction with No. 105, 'Lady Reading Book', and No. 110, 'Lady Fastening Shoe'. The copper plates are still in existence, and show these three engravings all together on one plate, thereby enabling the three different prints to be produced with one operation. In one size only and not produced on ware.

£60 — £80

No. 102 The Toilette

A very attractive lid from the factory of F. & R. Pratt, only produced in one size. This print is known on wares such as tobacco jars, etc. A variety of this lid has a fancy decorative border, and another variety has the name misspelt as 'The Tiolette'. One variety is known without the name and carrying a wide gold band. Copied from a painting by Casper Netscher, 'Interior of Dutch house' (see illustration).

With correct spelling. . . . .   £100—£150
With title misspelt. . . . .   £100—£150
With wide gold band and no title. . .   £300—£500
Tobacco jars. . . . .   £150 plus

No. 103 The Packman

Almost certainly produced by J. Ridgway, Bates & Co., at the Cauldon factory, in the mid 1850s. Two varieties of this lid are known, one has no wording round the print, the other has the words 'Bucks Venetian Pomade' in the upper section, and in the lower is the address, '48 Threadneedle Street'. The lid with no wording round the print is seen in two sizes, medium and small. Taken from a painting by J. Nash, as used in Sir Walter Scott's *Kenilworth*.

With wording	*£80—£100*
Without wording	*£50—£75*

No. 104 Reflection in Mirror

Presumed to have been produced at the Burslem factory of T.J. & J. Mayer. As mentioned previously, items produced by this factory at this period, i.e. c.1855, are not used on any kind of ware. Details are the same as lids Nos. 97, 98 and 99, and the name of Henry Trinder, of 75 Watling Street, St. Paul's, London is printed on the underside of a number of these lids (see left). Either with a fancy border or a white surround.

Either variety £125 — £200

No. 105 Lady Reading Book

All details as No. 101 'The Mirror', and No. 110, 'Lady Fastening Shoe', except that this print is the only one of the three to be recorded in the factory book of pulls (Appendix II).

Lid	*£60—£80*
Complete with tall pot . .	*£100—£125*

Above: These colourful vases are really sauce bottles and it is surprising that more were not preserved for posterity. Also included are two vases showing Chinese junks, both wonderful examples of the art of multicolour printing.

Below: Specially for the smokers. Tobacco jars and spill vases. Utilitarian items which not only serve a useful purpose but are also attractive to the eye.

No. 106 Lady with Hawk

A Pratt lid of which the copper plates are still in existence, also recorded in the factory book of pulls (Appendix II). Two varieties are known: the lady's dress is either striped or plain, and some of the lids have an extra white border.

Either variety £60 — £80

No. 107 Lady with Guitar

There is no certainty as to the factory of origin, but from the similarity of this lid with Nos. 115, 120, 121 and 127, it is thought that all these lids were produced at the Cauldon factory by J. Ridgway, Bates & Co., in the 1850s. This is borne out by the similarity with acknowledged Cauldon lids and the fact that these prints are not seen on ware, which is the usual pattern with lids produced at Cauldon at this period. Varieties will be seen with or without the wording 'Cold Cream of Roses' at the foot. Two sizes are known, medium and small, with the medium size having a raised floral border and the smaller one printed to the edge of the lid, with no border.

Small with lettering	*£75—£100*
Small without lettering	*£40—£60*
Medium with lettering	*£50—£75*
Medium without lettering	*£30—£50*

No. 108 The Wooer

Possibly produced by J. Ridgway, Bates & Co., at Cauldon. Only known on lids, in two sizes, medium and small.

Either size £150 — £250

No. 109 Lady, Boy and Mandoline
A Pratt lid produced 1850-60, the copper plates are still preserved and it is recorded in the factory record book. Produced in two sizes, medium and small, and not seen on any ware.

Either size £75 — £100

No. 110 Lady Fastening Shoe
All details as for Nos. 101 and 105, in one size only and not known on ware.

£60 — £80

No. 111 Lady Brushing Hair
From F. & R. Pratt c.1850, the plates still in existence show not only 'Lady Brushing Hair', but also No. 118 'The Trysting Place' and No. 119 'The Lovers' together on one set of copper plates. Engraved on the reverse of the plates is the name 'Jenny Lind'. Two varieties of this lid are known and recorded in the factory book, one with a purple bodice and one with a white bodice.

With purple bodice	*£100—£120*
With white bodice	*£120—£150*

No. 112 The Spanish Lady

Assumed to be Pratt due to its similarity with lids known to be Pratt, although no records exist to show any definite identification. The shape and style are very similar to lid No. 102, 'The Toilette'. A painting by G. Herbert entitled 'The Bull-fight' was used by J. Austin to execute his engraving for this print.

> Plain surround £250—£400
> Complete with mottled pot £400 plus

No. 113 Fruit and Statue Piece

Most likely produced at Cauldon during the period J. Austin was employed, c.1860. The original drawing by Austin is still in existence and shows a difference from the lid, in that the glass case seen on the lid encloses a figure, whereas the drawing (below) shows a vase under the cover. An unusually shaped convex lid to fit a shaped pot. No copper plates are preserved, but curiously the print is shown in the factory record book (Appendix II), which leads one to speculate how the print can be shown, when no copper plates are available for such records.

> Lid only £150—£250
> Lid and pot complete £300—£400

No. 114 The Matador

Most probably Mayers owing to the similarity with other Mayer lids, e.g. No. 135, 'Grand Exhibition 1851'. One size only and not on any item of ware.
> £300 — £500

No. 115 The Garden Terrace

All details as stated for No. 107, 'Lady with guitar'. A very similar lid to No. 120, 'The rose garden'. They both have a variety with a raised floral border showing a beehive within the surround.

Without raised border and beehive   *£100—£150*
With raised border and beehive   *£125—£200*

No. 116 Jenny Lind

Only seen on lids, there is no definite proof as to the factory of origin. Mayers has been suggested because of certain potter's marks, but the colour has certain similarities with lids produced by Ridgways when at Cauldon.

This famous soprano was born at Stockholm in 1820 and the story is that, when she was eight years of age, the maid of a famous dancer of the period, Mlle. Lundberg, heard Jenny singing to her cat and, as a result, persuaded her mistress to encourage Jenny Lind's mother to arrange singing lessons for the girl. (See also Appendix V.)

Lid only . . . . *£500—£800*
Complete with gold scroll borders and base to match . . . . . .   *P.B.N.*

No. 117 The Tryst

Thought to have been produced by T.J. & J. Mayer, and is only known to have been produced on lids. In one size only.

£100 — £150

No. 118 The Trysting Place

Details as for No. 111, 'Lady Brushing Hair'. Several varieties are known, fancy border with white surround, line border with white surround, or gold line border. Not used on ware.

Any variety £60 — £100

No. 119 The Lovers

Details as for Nos. 111, 'Lady Brushing Hair', and 118, 'The Trysting Place'. There are a number of varieties, fancy border, line border, gold line border, and also printed to the edge of the lid. Occasionally found on ware such as the illustrated spill jar, which has the Pratt marking of a crown and the wording, 'Manufacturers to H.R.H. Prince Albert', which proves manufacture before 1861.

Any variety . . . . £60—£100
Complete on tall pot £80—£120
Spill jar . . . . £50—£80

No. 120 The Rose Garden

Details as listed for Nos. 107, 'Lady with Guitar', and 115, 'The Garden Terrace'. Lids will be seen either with the wording 'Ross & Sons' or 'G.T. Jerram'.

Without raised border and beehive £100—£150
With raised border and beehive £125—£200

No. 121 The Ornamental Garden

Very similar to the lids No. 115 and 120. The wording 'Ross & Sons, 119 & 120 Bishopgate St., London' is contained within the print, with the wording 'Cold cream of roses' at the top.

Without raised border and beehive	*£100—£150*
With raised border and beehive	*£125—£200*

No. 122 Meditation

No definite attribution as to factory of origin, but presumed to have been produced by T.J. & J. Mayer. Wording similar to No. 5 'The Prowling Bear', with the addition of the words 'Royal Circassian Cream'. Seen on lids in one size only.

P.B.N.

No. 123 Musical Trio

An early lid, thought to have been manufactured by Ridgways at Cauldon. The usual pattern applies, no ware is seen bearing this print, which is to be expected with all these early Cauldon lids. Produced in two sizes, medium and small, also several varieties, double line border, pink border, gold line, and another variety has the wording 'Bucks Venetian Pomade. 48 Threadneedle St.'.

Without wording	*£60—£100*
With wording	*£80—£120*

No. 124 Bay of Naples

A very well produced lid which has every appearance of being manufactured at Cauldon during the Ridgway and J. Austin period. The wording, 'Prepared by G.T. Jerram, late Whitaker & Co., 69 Hatton Garden London', supports this attribution, as lids were produced for this cosmetic manufacturer by J. Ridgway. The wording 'Naples Shaving Paste' is seen within the top section of the print. W. Callow was the artist responsible for this painting, from which J. Austin probably made his copy (see illustration). The original was purchased by Queen Victoria in 1852 and was added to her collection of paintings in Osborne House. Unrecorded on ware and of one size only.

Gold line border	*£250—£400*
Extra wide gold band	*£500—£700*

No. 125 Gothic Archway

Origin of factory unknown, although the colouring and style lead one to assume that this particular lid was produced by T.J. & J. Mayer, as were so many of these pots made to contain cosmetics. Two sizes of this lid are known, medium and small, and some lids have the wording 'Cold Cream' showing in the top section. Several different varieties of borders are known, either printed to the edge of the lid, with a white surround or with a narrow ornamental border. This item was also produced complete with lid and pot, both having a mottled surface, and was produced for the firm of 'Maws', possibly the firm of S. Maw & Sons, Aldersgate St., London.

With wording	*P.B.N.*
Without wording	*P.B.N.*
Mottled lid and pot complete	*P.B.N.*

No. 126 Bunch of Cherries

Certainly produced by Mayers, the usual number, possibly a workman's mark, can be seen on the underside. Only produced in one size, and again, not seen on ware. This lid has the wording 'Rimmels Cherry Tooth paste' round the perimeter. A recent find is a very similar lid, except that the word 'Coral' is substituted for the word 'Cherry' and the illustration shows shells instead of cherries.

Cherry tooth paste	*£40—£75*
Coral tooth paste	*£100—£150*

No. 127 The Circassian

All details as for No. 107, 'Lady with Guitar'. One size only and not found on ware. The wording shows the manufacturer to be G.T. Jerram, late Whitaker & Co., 69 Hatton Garden London, who produced Circassian Cream, obviously produced after Jerram succeeded Whitaker. No. 14, 'Bear in a Ravine', shows only Whitaker's name and address, whereas this lid, No. 127, and also No. 124, 'Bay of Naples', show both the names of G.T. Jerram and Whitaker.

£100 — £150

No. 128 Albert Edward, Prince of Wales, and Princess Alexandra of Denmark

No. 130 The Bee-hive

No definite evidence is available to determine the factory of origin of these three lids. No. 128, 'Albert Edward Prince of Wales, and Princess Alexandra of Denmark', indicates the date of production, because this item obviously would be produced either during the period of engagement or their wedding in 1863. No. 129, 'Royal Arms & Allied Flags', by showing the allies' flags as in the Crimean war, also suggests the date of production.

No. 128 P.B.N.
No. 129 P.B.N.
No. 130 P.B.N.

No. 129 Royal Arms and Allied Flags of the Crimea

Floral Subjects

This particular section has been sadly neglected in previous writings on underglaze colour printing. This is understandable, as records are almost non-existent. However, it is now possible to name the factory of origin of a number of these lids and, wherever possible, an attribution has been made.

This section also lends itself to the problem of whether lids are genuine or not. Obviously, experience is the best criterion, but, if in any doubt, perhaps the following tips may help.

1. Always check to see if the subject is illustrated in this Guide.
2. Pass the hand gently over the surface of the object; if underglazed printed, it will feel quite smooth; if painted or printed overglaze, this can be felt.

No. 131/1
Factory unknown.
£100 — £200

No. 131/2
Certainly from Pratt, very similar to Nos. 131/3 and 131/9, which are recorded in the factory book of pulls. One of these lids was recently dug up on the factory site. A variety can be found with screw top.

Without screw top	*£40—£60*
With screw top	*£60—£100*
Screw top complete with base	*£80—£120*

No. 131/3
Details as No. 131/2. Copper plates still preserved, which show not only this engraving, but also Nos. 131/4, 131/9, 131/12A, all engraved on one set of copper plates (Appendix I). See also factory book of pulls (Appendix II). Screw top lids are known.

Without screw top	*£40—£60*
With screw top	*£60—£100*
Screw top complete with base	*£80—£120*

No. 131/4

Known to be Pratt/Cauldon. See details of No. 131/3. Apparently, a different style of printing was adopted for the flower lids. It was usual to complete the print by the addition of an outline plate but examination of the existing plates shows an extra green colour, with no outline.

£50 — £80

No. 131/5

No definite proof of factory of origin. A very popular subject which was produced in three sizes, over a number of years, confirmation of which is seen by reference to the addresses shown on the lids. Apparently Piesse & Lubin, who used these pots, continued to use this engraving each time they moved by changing only the address: 2 Bond Street, London, 28 South Molton Street, London and 189 Regent Street, London W.1. This latter lid is sometimes seen complete on a shaped pot. A very small size with no name and address is shown and listed as No. 131/19. Thought to be Pratt by the style of printing.

Medium size	*£30—£50*
Small size	*£40—£60*
Complete on shaped pot	*£75—£100*

No. 131/6

No. 131/7

The two lids 131/6 and 131/7 are very similar, the only difference being that the vase seen on both prints differs. 131/6 shows the vase with a ribbed body, with No. 131/7 showing the vase with a mottled body. The lids are very attractive, with an unusually high domed top, and very often are still found complete on a tall marbled pot. No records exist which show the factory of manufacture but there appears to be no doubt at all that they were produced by F. & R. Pratt. This assumption can be made with the utmost confidence, when these lids and pots are compared to exactly similar lids and pots which are definitely known to have been produced by F. & R. Pratt; e.g., No. 311 'I see you my boy', No. 345 'Girl with grapes', No. 348 'Peasant boys' and No. 360 'A letter from the diggings'. J. Gosnell & Co., London, was the manufacturer for whom they were made and, quite often, this name is seen either printed or impressed on the base of the pot.

Lid only　　　　　*£80—£120*
Complete with pot　*£125—£200*

No. 131/8

A quite rare and beautifully produced lid and pot from the Mayer factory. Round the sunflower on the lids is the wording 'James King's Sunflower Pomatum', whilst the pot has a decorative scene marked 'An old world garden'.

Without pot　*P.B.N.*
With pot　　*P.B.N.*

No. 131/9
All details as listed for Nos. 131/3, 131/4 and 131/12A.
Lid only £40—£60
Screw top complete with base £75—£100

No. 131/10

This print was used not only on lids but it is also seen as the decorative centre-piece of plates and other items of dessert ware. Probably produced by T.J. & J. Mayer.

Lids £40—£60
Plates or Comports £30—£50

No. 131/11

No. 131/12

No facts or records exist to attribute either of these lids to one particular factory.
No. 131/11 £40—£60
No. 131/12 £40—£60

No. 131/12A
See all details as listed for Nos. 131/3/4/9. Also refer to notes on the list of existing copper plates from the Pratt factory (Appendix I). A later edition of this lid has been seen with a blue border.

Without border	*P.B.N.*
With blue border	*£40—£60*

No. 131/13
A lid from F. & R. Pratt produced in several varieties; either convex or flat surface, complete with shaped pot, with green ground border complete with tall green pot, or with malachite border.

Flat or convex	*£40—£60*
Complete with shaped pot	*£80—£120*
Complete on tall pot	*£80—£120*
With malachite border	*£120—£200*

No. 131/14
Possibly a Pratt lid due to the similarity of the raised floral border to Nos. 107, 115 and 120.
£50 — £75

No. 131/15
An oblong box and top from F. & R. Pratt as listed in the records.

Complete with box	*£60—£100*
Lid only	*£50—£80*

No. 131/16   No. 131/17

Two small lids produced by F. & R. Pratt which are practically identical, except that No. 131/17 shows a little more foliage.

Either lid   *£30—£50*
Complete with pot   *£40—£60*

No. 131/18

Possibly Pratt, but no definite proof. A small lid, similar to 131/16 and 131/17.

     Lid only   *£30—£50*
     Complete with pot   *£40—£60*

No. 131/19

All details as for No. 131/5. When on small shaped pot, the name of Piesse & Lubin is printed round the centre of the pot.

   Lid only   *£60—£100*
   Complete on shaped pot   *£100—£150*

No. 131/20   **No. 131/21**   **No. 131/22**

These three lids were all produced by F. & R. Pratt, as records show. No. 21 is a small lid similar to Nos. 131/16-131/19.

No. 20	*£30—£50*	*No. 21*	*£30—£50*	*No. 22*	*£30—£50*
Complete with pot	*£40—£60*	*Complete with pot*	*£40—£60*	*Complete with pot*	*£40—£60*

No. 131/23
Possibly by F. & R. Pratt. Two sizes are known.
Lid only £25—£40
Complete with pot £30—£50

No. 131/24
An attractive lid by F. & R. Pratt.
Lid only £60—£100
Complete with pot £80—£120

No. 131/25

No. 131/26

No. 131/27

No. 131/28

No definite proof of factory of origin for these lids. Nos. 26 and 27 are identical except that No. 26 has the wording 'J. Grossmith & Co. 85 Newgate St. London' round the border. The address shown was the business address of J. Grossmith & Co. from 1835 until 1888, after which they moved to 29 Newgate Street.

131/25	£40—£60
131/26	£100—£150
131/27	£100—£150
131/28	£60—£80

Floral Subjects

No. 131/29
An advertising lid for 'J.S. Higgins' comprising a floral
border which has also been used on dessert ware.
£100 — £200

No. 131/30
Previously titled 'Flowers, vase & mirror', thought to
have been produced by T.J. & J. Mayer. May be found
in two sizes, either small or medium.
Either size £100 — £120

No. 131/31
An unusually shaped vase thought to be T.J.
& J. Mayer.
£60 — £80

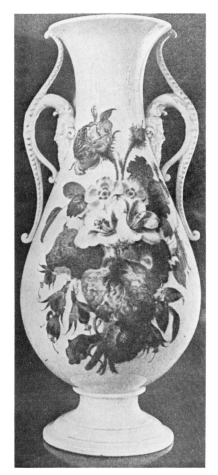

85

No. 131/32

No. 131/32A

Almost certainly produced by T.J. & J. Mayer, as the usual Mayer
workman's number is printed on the base.
Either variety £25 — £40

No. 131/33
This print has only been seen on a tea-pot stand.
£30 — £50

No. 131/34
A similar lid to No. 131/15, almost certainly by F. & R.
Pratt.

Lid only	*£50—£80*
Complete with box	*£60—£100*

No. 131/35
Dessert ware produced by F. & R. Pratt c.1860.
£25 — £50

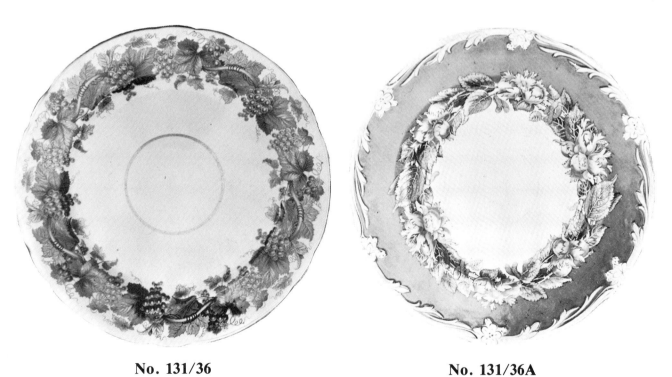

No. 131/36   **No. 131/36A**

Dessert ware made by Mayer & Elliott c.1858-61.
£25 — £50

A number of colourful dressing table items used by the ladies of the period when preparing their toilette. The boxes contained powders, rouge, creams, etc.

Exhibition Subjects

Much interest is shown with all exhibition lids but more particularly with the Exhibition of 1851 (see also Appendix V). The Great Exhibition was primarily responsible for the arousing interest in and demand for all items of underglaze multicolour printing, as seen on ware of the period. Amongst the firms who displayed this new method of colour printing were Ridgway, Pratt and Mayer.

The following extracts are taken directly from the official catalogue and show which items these three firms had on display.

John Ridgway & Co., Cauldon Place, Staffordshire

"Improved fine vitreous earthenware, consisting of specimens of the various articles in table and dessert suites; also, toilet and tea ware, coloured and printed."

T.J. & J. Mayer, Dale Hall Pottery, Longport, Burslem, Staffordshire

"Specimens of earthenware. Table ware in various patterns, and printed in a variety of colours. Various specimens of enamelled and gilt toilette and dessert ware. Various designs for meat pots, printed in colours, under the glaze.

Advertising tiles, of various designs, printed in colours."

F. & R. Pratt

"Terra-cotta model for a timepiece, 'Paris and Helen'.
Two Etruscan vases, with figures from 'Flaxman's Iliad'.
Porous water-coolers, plain and in enamelled colours.
Earthenware, printed in various colours, under glaze, after pictures in the Vernon Gallery, &c.

Dessert ware, with the following subjects:—
'The Last In', W. Mulready, R.A.
'Highland Music', Sir E. Landseer, R.A.
'The Blind Fiddler', Sir D. Wilkie, R.A.
'The Truant', T. Webster, R.A.
'The Hop Queen', W.T. Witherington, R.A.
'Cottage Children', T. Gainsborough, R.A.
Bread platter, and cheese dish, picture and frame, with scripture subject by H. Warren.
Two pictures printed in colours, under glaze, in earthenware frames. A variety of box covers, and pair of ornamental vases, in the same style.
Dessert ware, Etruscan shapes, in white and gold.
A variety of printed and enamelled dinner ware.
A mazarine blue jar, ornamented in gold.

These subjects are executed under the glaze by the ordinary process of 'bisque' printing, each colour is produced from a separate engraving, and the 'transfer' required to be carefully registered."

The catalogue then continues by giving a description of how this process was developed. Details of this process have been given in the Introduction, but a further elaboration will not be out of place, by quoting the actual details, as given by Messrs. F. & R. Pratt, to the Commissioners of the Exhibition.

"The process of bisque firing is as follows:— The ware being finished from the hand of the potter, is brought by him upon boards to the 'green-house', so called from its being the receptacle for ware in the 'green' or unfired state. It is here gradually dried for the ovens: when ready, it is carried to the 'sagger-house', in immediate connexion with the oven in which it is to be fired, and here it is placed in the 'saggers': these are boxes made of a peculiar kind of clay (a native marl), previously fired, and fusible at the heat required for the ware, and of form suited to the articles they are to contain. A little dry pounded flint is scattered between them, of china and sand of earthenware, to prevent adhesion. The purpose of the sagger is to protect the ware from the flames and smoke, and also for its security from breakage, as in the clay state it is exceedingly brittle, and when dry, or what is called 'white', requires great care in the handling.

A plate sagger will hold twenty places, placed one on the other, of earthenware; but china plates are fired separately in 'setters' made of their respective forms. The 'setters' for china plates and dishes answer the same purpose as the 'saggers', and are made of the same clay. They take in one dish or plate each, and are 'reared' in the oven in 'bungs' one on the other.

The hovels in which the ovens are built form a very peculiar and striking feature of the pottery towns, and forcibly arrest the attention and excite the surprise of the stranger, resembling as they closely do a succession of gigantic bee-hives. They are constructed of bricks, about 40 feet diameter, and 35 feet high, with an aperture at the top for the escape of the smoke. The 'ovens' are of a similar form, about 22 feet diameter, and from 18 to 21 feet high, heated by fire-places, or 'mouths', about nine in number, built externally around them. Flues in connexion with these converge under the bottom of the oven to a central opening, drawing the flames to this point, where they enter the oven: other flues, termed 'bags', pass up the internal sides to the height of about four feet, thus conveying the flames to the upper part.

When 'setting in' the oven, the firemen enter by an opening in the side, carrying the saggers with the ware placed as described: these are piled one upon another from bottom to top of the oven, care being taken to arrange them so that they may receive the heat (which varies in different parts) most suited to the articles they contain. This being continued till the oven is filled, the aperture is then bricked up: the firing of earthenware bisque continues sixty hours, and of china forty-eight.

The quantity of coals necessary for a 'bisque' oven is from 16 to 20 tons; for a 'ghost' oven from 4½ to 6 tons.

The ware is allowed to cool for two days, when it is drawn in the state technically termed 'biscuit', or bisque, and is then ready for 'glazing', except when required for printing, or a common style of painting, both of which processes are done on the 'bisque' prior to being 'glazed'.''

No. 133 Grand International Buildings of 1851

A lid from T.J. & J. Mayer, which was registered in advance of the opening date, i.e. May 1st, 1851. Messrs. Crosse & Blackwell registered the design on October 23rd, 1850, with the name 'The Glass Palace'; this was later deleted. The wording was altered to read, 'The Grand International Building of 1851, For the Exhibition of Art and Industry of all Nations'. Not known on ware but was originally seen as the frontispiece to 'The Great Exhibition Polka 1851'.

Double line border . . . . £50—£75
Gold band . . . . £100—£150
With 'The Glass Palace' wording . . P.B.N.

No. 134 Exhibition Buildings 1851

There are several varieties of this lid, which was a product of F. & R. Pratt. The list of copper plates shows that separate engravings were made for lids and those used for vases. In the engraving for the vases it was found necessary to reduce the size. This was done by omitting two figures on horseback, two figures in the foreground and several figures from the mid-distance, and was usually referred to as the 'Princess Christian' vase. Varieties of this vase have been seen without the coat of arms. A later edition, on a pot-lid, made use of the engraved copper plate as used on the vase.

Large, with acorn border	*£120—£175*
Medium, no border and gold line	*£100—£150*
Medium, figures omitted	*£80—£100*
Vases	*£100 plus*

No. 135 Grand Exhibition 1851

From T.J. & J. Mayer, often seen with the usual Mayer number printed on the underside; in this case it is 7. Only the one size and has not been found on any kind of ware.

£50 — £75

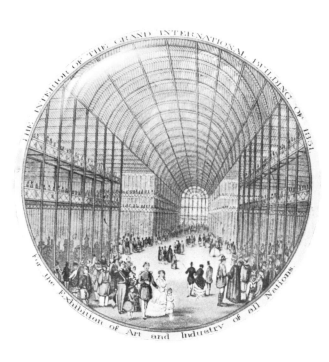

No. 136 The Interior of the Grand International Building of 1851

Produced by T.J. & J. Mayer in two varieties. One variety has the title within the white surround border. The rarer variety has no title and the transept is extended to measure an eighth of an inch only. Often numbered 7 on the underside.

With title	*£75—£100*
Without title	*£100—£150*

No. 137 The Crystal Palace

Produced by F. & R. Pratt in one size only. Similar to No. 138.

£75 — £100

No. 138 Interior View of Crystal Palace

Produced by F. & R. Pratt in one size only, the title shown in the top section. This design was also used on tea-plates.

Lids	*£75—£100*
Plates	*£30—£50*

No. 139 Crystal Palace (Interior)

A similar lid to Nos. 137 and 138 but, in this instance, the manufacturer was T.J. & J. Mayer. One size only.

£75 — £100

**No. 140   The Great Exhibition of 1851
(Opening Ceremony)**

**No. 141   The Great Exhibition of 1851
(Closing Ceremony)**

Two lids from T.J. & J. Mayer which form an excellent pair. No. 140 shows Queen Victoria performing the opening ceremony on May 1st, 1851, and No. 141 shows Prince Albert conducting the closing ceremony on October 15th, 1851. One size only is known.

No. 142   New York Exhibition 1853

Produced by T.J. & J. Mayer, in one size only. Great care must be exercised when acquiring this lid; many late reissues are known (see Introduction). After opening on Juiy 14th, 1853, the building was destroyed by fire on October 5th, 1853.

Early issue	*£400—£500*
Late issues	*£15—£30*

No. 143   Dublin Industrial Exhibition 1853

A large lid in one size only, produced by F. & R. Pratt to commemorate the opening of the Dublin Exhibition on May 12th, 1853. Only known on lids.

£50 — £75

No. 144 International Exhibition 1862

No definite proof of factory, but probably produced at Cauldon. This particular exhibition was situated in Kensington, opening on May 1st, 1862, and closing on November 1st, 1862. One size only and not on ware.

£60 — £80

No. 145 L'Exposition Universelle de 1867

Produced by F. & R. Pratt on the occasion of the opening of the Paris exhibition on April 1st, 1867. Only in one size, with later issues seen with an extra white surround. Some lids, like the one shown here, have the word 'illustree' included in the title. Not known on any kind of ware.

Either variety £30 — £50

No. 146 The Administration Building
Worlds Fair, Chicago 1893

A monochrome lid which is included in this section merely to complete all the exhibition subjects. Will be seen in two different varieties of colour, either black/grey or reddish brown. Usually in medium size, but a larger version is known by the addition of extra borders. Possibly produced by F. & R. Pratt after the death of J. Austin. .

Either variety £80 — £120

No. 147 Philadelphia Exhibition 1876

Several varieties of this subject are known to have been
produced by the factory of F. & R. Pratt. The exhibition
was designed to celebrate the centenary of American
Independence. Records show two sizes of the oblong
variety and three sizes of the circular one. The oblong
variety omits the two ladies in the foreground and the
carriage and pair with passengers. A set of three jugs is
known to be in existence, with the oblong print on each
jug.

Round variety   £30—£50
Oblong variety   £40—£60

No. 148 Paris Exhibition 1878

Another F. & R. Pratt lid. It was commented at the
time, that this exhibition was the largest ever recorded,
the site being 66 acres. Probably the exhibition was held
to celebrate the recovery of France after the Franco-
Prussian War of 1870-71. Only in one size and not
found on ware.

£30 — £50

Portrait Subjects

No. 149 England's Pride

Two issues of this lid are known. The preserved copper plates (Appendix I) show a black background, but the earlier and more scarce edition was produced with a green background. This makes for a considerable difference in price. Both editions were produced by F. & R. Pratt, the first possibly c.1850, with the later one c.1860-70. There are two sizes, medium and large (by the addition of a fancy border). Unrecorded on ware.

Green background	*£150—£200*
Black background	*£50—£75*

No. 150 Queen Victoria on Balcony

A rare print from T.J. & J. Mayer, produced some time after the Baxter print titled 'England's Queen' was published in 1848. The lid and the print being alike, the lid has always been said to be 'in reverse to the Baxter print'. This is not strictly true; the only part in reverse is the marble pillar on the balcony and Windsor Castle in the distance. The figure of Her Majesty is exactly as shown in the Baxter print. Not used on ware. Two sizes are known, medium and large with fancy rosette design border. The Baxter print, in common with the large size lid, shows the pavement in blue, whilst the medium lid has the pavement in red.

Medium size	*£80—£120*
Large size	*£120—£180*
Large size complete with	
domed top and marbled pot	*P.B.N.*

No. 151 Queen Victoria with Orb and Sceptre
A similar lid to No. 150, produced by the same firm,
T.J. & J. Mayer, at approximately the same period.
Large   £80—£120
Medium   £80—£120

No. 152 Queen Victoria and the Prince Consort
Almost certainly produced by F. & R. Pratt prior to the death of Prince Albert in 1861. A rare lid, produced in one
size only. Tea-plates with this print were produced much later. The registration mark on the underside shows that
these commemorative plates were first registered on September 25th, 1868.
Lids £100 — £150   Plates £30 — £50

No. 153 The Late Prince Consort

Produced by F. & R. Pratt as a commemorative item after the death of Prince Albert in 1861 (see Appendix V). A very popular item, but has not been seen on ware. One size only.

£30 — £50

No. 154 Queen Victoria and Albert Edward

The manufacturer of this lid is not definitely known but evidence points to the possibility of it being produced by the Cauldon factory c.1849-50. A very unusual lid, the Queen's arms seem rather elongated and out of proportion. Possibly a little hand-colouring on the back of the chair.

£175 — £300

No. 155 Albert Edward, Prince of Wales and Princess Alexandra

Definitely a Mayer lid, as the markings show on the underside. One size only and not yet found on ware. It has been suggested that this lid was produced to commemorate the wedding of H.R.H. Prince of Wales to Princess Alexandra in 1863.

£100 — £150

No. 156 Napoleon III and Empress Eugenie

Most probably a Cauldon lid produced during the period when the factory was owned by J. Ridgway, Bates and Co., 1855-58. Again we see the pattern of early Cauldon lids not being included in the list of combined Cauldon/Pratt lids. This occurs so often that it is impossible not to draw the conclusion that the early Cauldon items did not receive the same preferential treatment as Pratt.

£125 — £175

**No. 157 Albert Edward, Prince of Wales
and Princess Alexandra
on their Marriage in 1863**

As the title suggests, a lid made by F. & R. Pratt to commemorate the wedding of H.R.H. Prince of Wales and Princess Alexandra of Denmark. An interesting detail on this lid is the Prince of Wales' feathers at the top, with the Danish coat of arms at the foot, represented by the elephant and howdah. A popular lid which was reissued over the years; later issues can be distinguished by the addition of an outer Greek-key border. One size only and unrecorded on ware.

Early edition   £50—£75
Late edition   £30—£50

The popularity of 'The Iron Duke' was never more clearly expressed than in the production of the following lids which show twelve different portraits.

**No. 158 Wellington with Cocked Hat
(no lettering)**

**No. 159 Wellington with Cocked Hat
(lettering)**

Both lids were produced by T.J. & J. Mayer, the only differences being the wording round the border of No. 159 which gives details of the birth and death of the Duke, and the background colour to No. 158 being of a greenish colour, plus a different design border. It appears that No. 158 was the earlier lid, with No. 159 being adapted from the same copper plates after the death of the Duke of Wellington, by giving biographical details round the border.

Without lettering £250 — £350   *With lettering £250 — £350*

Wellington (with clasped hands)

A series of four different varieties of this lid, produced by T.J. & J. Mayer c.1850. This series was probably issued before the Duke's death in 1852. No reference is made to his death on September 14th, 1852.

No. 160. Medium size, yellow inner border with scrolls and red dots, laurel leaf outer border with red bow at foot. Suspended from the Duke's neck is the 'Order of the Golden Fleece' and the title is shown beneath the portrait.

£80 — £120

No. 160A. Medium size, very similar to No. 160 except that the 'Order of the Golden Fleece' is deleted.
£75 — £100

No. 160B. Large size, additional laurel leaf border with red berries added, otherwise as No. 160A.
£75 — £100

No. 160C. Large size, similar to 160B, no title shown and colour omitted from berries, also the bow at the foot, which is red in 160, 160A and 160B, is coloured blue.

£80 — £120

The Late Duke of Wellington
Obit. Sept. 14th 1852

A series of lids produced by F. & R. Pratt, to commemorate the death of the Duke in 1852, at his residence, Walmer Castle.

No. 161. A large lid showing the Duke (without sash) sitting in a chair, surrounded by a laurel wreath border with wording as the title, an outer border designed to represent coloured marble. This lid was the first issue.
£80 — £120

No. 161A. A large lid, as No. 161, but showing the Duke with a sash over his shoulder, the marbled border is of a reddish colour.
£80 — £120

No. 161B. A medium size lid, exactly as No. 161A, with the marbled border omitted (a later issue).
£75 — £100

No. 161C. A large lid similar to No. 161A, with a malachite border replacing the marbled one.
Complete with malachite base P.B.N.

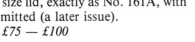

No. 162 Field Marshall the Duke of Wellington

A Pratt item which is different from Nos. 161-161C, in that it is signed by J. Austin. Similar to No. 161, except that the Duke is shown sitting on a couch instead of a chair. Possibly adapted from a miniature painted by D'Orsay (see above right).

P.B.N.

No. 163 Funeral of the Late Duke of Wellington

A lid produced by T.J. & J. Mayer to commemorate the death of the Duke of Wellington. Obviously derived from the same source as the Baxter print (see above right) with the same title, as both prints are identical. This lid is one of the many reissues which were produced up to and including the 1960s by Kirkhams (see Appendix III).

Early lids   *£250—£350*
Reissue lids   *£15—£30*

No. 164 Tria Juncta in Uno

'Three united in one', the title of this print shows the three monarchs who were allied against Russia in the Crimean War, 1854-56. Produced in two sizes, medium and large, with the larger size having a very decorative scroll border. The name Robert Feast, 15 & 16, Pavement, Finsbury Square, London, is printed on the underside. This firm used the pots from T.J. & J. Mayer for their potted meats. They also used containers, generally referred to as vases, for relishes and sauces, which have a similar inscription on the base.

Large size	*£150—£200*
Medium size	*£150—£200*
Heightened in gold	*£200—£300*
Vases	*£150 plus*

Two lids, in attractive gilt frames, with portraits of Sir Robert Peel and Prince Albert.

Two of the scarcest lids known, the reason being that only a limited number would have been made during the period of the 1876 Exhibition in Philadelphia, for the firm of H.P. & W.C. Taylor of Philadelphia.

No. 165 Alma
A companion lid to No. 164 also produced by T.J. & J. Mayer. The same inscription is printed on the underside. The print shows four of the generals in command at the time of the Battle of the Alma, 1854: Lord Raglan and the Duke of Cambridge (British), Marshall St. Arnaud (French) and Omar Pasha (Turkish).

Large	*£150—£200*
Medium	*£150—£200*
Vases	*£150 plus*

No. 166 Balaklava, Inkerman, Alma

Another Crimean War lid by T.J. & J. Mayer, similar to the two previous lids Nos. 164 and 165. An interesting detail of this lid shows the Earl of Cardigan, who was in command of the ill-fated charge of the Light Brigade, wearing a busby. The three prints Nos. 164, 165 and 166 were continued for several years on items other than lids, e.g. the jug illustrated is dated 1868.

Lids	*£150—£200*
Plaques	*£100—£150*
Jugs	*£75—£100*
Other items	*P.B.N.*

No. 167 and 167A Admiral Sir Charles Napier, C.B.

Another of the very popular Crimean subjects by T.J. & J. Mayer and used by the firm of Robert Feast for their potted meats etc. Two sizes are known — medium and large. The medium has no border or title and a green background. The large size has a decorative rope and anchor border, with the title at the foot. A tile has been seen with the large print and border; on the reverse is printed 'Specimen of printed earthenware, 1854', also showing the royal coat of arms and the wording 'T.J. & J. Mayer (Patent) Dale Hall Pottery, Longport'. Sir Charles Napier was in command of the Baltic fleet in 1854, and until his death in 1860 he was M.P. for Southwark.

With border (167) £150 — £250   *Without border (167A) £150 — £200*   *Tile P.B.N.*

No. 168 Allied Generals

A Crimean War subject by F. & R. Pratt, and one of the lids which bears the signature of J. Austin. The registration mark seen at the foot, shows the date as December 29th, 1854. One size only, but in three varieties, laurel leaf border, heightened in gold or complete with gold flecked pot. The two generals shown are the English and French commanders-in-chief associated in the Crimean War.

Laurel leaf border   £40—£60
Heightened in gold   £150—£250
Gold flecked pot complete   P.B.N.

No. 169 Garibaldi

A lid produced by F. & R. Pratt, probably to celebrate the visit of Garibaldi to England in 1864. One size only, but has occasionally been seen on plates.

Lids £20 — £30   *Plates £15 — £25*

No. 170 Sir Robert Peel

F. & R. Pratt produced this lid in the early 1860s after the death of Sir Robert Peel in 1860, due to an accident whilst riding in Hyde Park. Several different varieties are known, mainly in the colour of the curtains. The title is seen on one of the books, also the signature of 'J.A. sc.' can be seen on another of the books. One lid only has been seen without the title.

Wheatear border	*£75—£100*
Malachite surround	*P.B.N.*
Without title on book	*P.B.N.*

No. 171 Peabody

A lid which is difficult to attribute to any one factory, as it is not listed in the surviving lists from Pratt/Cauldon (Appendix I) but is very similar in appearance to lids produced by Pratts in the late 1860s. George Peabody was an American subject who traded in London and gave away immense sums of money to the poor and homeless in the mid-1850s. He is remembered to this day for the privately built estates known as Peabody houses. One size only, but has been seen on plates. A very rare variety has a screw rim.

Lids	*£100—£150*
Plates	*£25—£40*
Screw rim variety	*P.B.N.*

No. 172 Harriet Beecher Stowe

Harriet Beecher Stowe visited England in 1853 and it is probable that T.J. & J. Mayer produced this lid to commemorate her visit. The title of her book 'Uncle Tom's Cabin' can be seen on the book resting on her lap. One size only and not seen on ware.

£250 — £350

No. 173 Felix Edwards Pratt

A rather late item from F. & R. Pratt, showing a head and shoulders portrait of Felix Pratt, possibly about 1875. Three items are recorded with this print: (a) a small rectangular plaque with a moulded border, produced as one piece, showing a green background to the portrait (later issues were produced with either a red or white background); (b) a medium sized lid with green background; (c) a small tea-plate with green background.

Plaque with green background	*£200—£300*
Plaque with red or white background	*£100—£150*
Lids	*£150—£200*
Plate	*£75—£100*

No. 174 The Blue Boy
See caption on page 112.

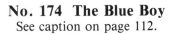

No. 174 The Blue Boy

A Pratt item which has been reissued many times since the first issues. The early lids, possibly produced c.1850-60, have a seaweed rim and were used on a pot, also with seaweed decoration (see illustration on page 111). Lids with a screw rim are contemporary with this variety but much rarer. Later lids have a white rim and are usually equal in colouring. Reissue lids were produced up to approximately 1920, but these items are very poor in colouring and are worth considerably less than the items mentioned above. Seen on other items of ware.

Screw top complete	*P.B.N.*	*Reissue*	*£15—£30*
Seaweed rim complete	*£250—£300*	*Plate*	*£25—£40*
White rim (late)	*£30—£40*	*Tile*	*£75—£100*

No. 175 Dr. Johnson

A lid in one size only, produced by F. & R. Pratt in the 1860s. Jesse Austin freely adapted his drawing for this lid from the painting by E.M. Ward (above right).

£20 — £30

Historic Buildings

No. 176 Buckingham Palace

A view of Buckingham Palace as in the early 1850s, by T.J. & J. Mayer. Buckingham Palace was built by John Sheffield, Duke of Buckingham, in 1698 (hence the name). The building was re-modelled by Nash in 1825 for George IV, and Queen Victoria made it her town residence when she came to the throne in 1837 (see also Appendix V).

Great care must be taken when acquiring this lid; many late issues are seen, and reissue lids made by Kirkham & Co. (Appendix III) are often offered for sale. These reissues are of little value.

Early issues	*£120—£175*
Late issues	*£25—£50*
Reissues	*£10—£20*

No. 177 Windsor Castle and St. George's Chapel

No definite proof of origin, but most probably made by J. Ridgway & Co. at the Cauldon factory c.1850. There are two sizes of this lid, 2½ins. and 2¾ins. The larger size sometimes has the wording 'Royal Windsor Toilet Cream' around the top, with 'S. Graftey & Co., Warwick Street, London' around the lower section.

Without wording £75 — £100   *With wording £100 — £125*

No. 178 Windsor Castle
or **Prince Albert (Hare Coursing)**

First produced by T.J. & J. Mayer in the 1850s and reissued for many years. Also seen on various wares. The copper plates, still in existence, have the name 'Albert' on the underside, obviously referring to the figure in the foreground.

Lids	*£80—£120*
Plaques	*£80—£120*
Mugs	*£50—£80*

No. 179 Drayton Manor

Another lid which was reissued by Kirkham's up to the 1960s. First issued by T.J. & J. Mayer contemporary with the Pratt 'Sir Robert Peel' (No. 170). Peel's residence was Drayton Manor. The early lids are much finer in texture than any produced at a later date. There are two sizes, medium or lage, and either with or without the title. Unrecorded on ware.

Either size.....	*£100—£150*
Reissue lid.....	*£20—£30*

No. 180 Windsor Park (Returning from Stag-Hunting)

A Pratt lid issued at the same time as the Baxter print of the same title, which was published in 1850 (see above right). One of the few lids produced with a raised moulded border, the raised section often with extra gold decoration.

£75 — £120

No. 181 Sandringham

Issued by F. & R. Pratt in the early 1860s, probably c.1862, the date this estate was purchased by the Prince of Wales. One size only, not seen on ware.

Double line border... £30—£50
Seaweed border..... £50—£75

No. 182 Osborne House

A Mayer lid produced in two size, medium and large, with the larger one showing a crown at the top centre. A later edition of the large variety can also be seen without the crown.

Either variety £50 — £75

No. 183 New Houses of Parliament Westminster

This large lid was issued in one size only by T.J. & J. Mayer to celebrate the opening of the New Parliament Buildings in 1852. Beware of late issues of this lid which are of little value.

The old Houses of Parliament were destroyed by fire in 1834. Workmen had been given instructions to burn the 'tally-sticks' which had accumulated in the store-rooms, but unfortunately the fire got completely out of hand.

'Tally-sticks' were hazel or willow sticks about 8ins. long with notches on them to represent sums of money. The stick was split into two, one half being a receipt and the exchequer keeping the other as a record of payments made. This was necessary because so many civil servants were unable either to read or write.

The use of these 'tallies' had been discontinued by an Act of Parliament in 1782, and by 1834 there was such an accumulation that it was decided to burn them with disasterous consequences. Temporary accommodation was provided over the years until the present building was opened in 1852, although it was not completed until 1857.

£150 — £200

No. 184 The Houses of Parliament
A small lid produced at an unknown factory c.1852.
£150 — £200

No. 185 St. Paul's Cathedral and River Pageant
A Pratt lid produced in two sizes, medium and large, in the early 1850s. The last recorded time that a Lord Mayor of London used this method of transport for the Lord Mayor's Show was November 9th, 1856.
Either size £50 — £80

No. 186 The Tower of London

This lid, and also Nos. 189, 192 and 195 all bear the wording 'Entered at Stationers Hall' (see Glossary, Registration). The factory of manufacture is unknown and was probably smaller than Mayer, Cauldon or Pratt. These lids are very rare, as only small quantities were issued. One size only, unrecorded on ware.

£125 — £175

No. 187 Strathfieldsay

Factory not known but presumed to be the same as the one who produced No. 234, 'Pet Rabbits', as the borders used are identical. This lid must not be confused with the following lid No. 188, 'Strathfieldsaye'. Two sizes known, medium and large. Not seen on ware.

Either size £75 — £100

No. 188 Strathfieldsaye

A large lid produced by F. & R. Pratt, showing the home of the Duke of Wellington in Hampshire. Other items have been seen with this print.

Lids £50 — £75   *Plates £15 — £30*

No. 189 Westminster Abbey
All details as for No. 186, 'The Tower of London'.
£125 — £175

No. 190 Albert Memorial
A medium-sized lid, probably from Bates, Elliott and Co. Other lids with similar appearance from this same factory are Nos. 192A and 194. Unrecorded on ware.
£40 — £60

No. 191 Albert Memorial
From F. & R. Pratt, this lid is rather late in period. The memorial to the Prince Consort was opened in 1872 and the statue was unveiled in 1876 (see also Appendix V). One size only and is seen either with or without the title. Not on ware.

£25 — £40

No. 192 St. Paul's Cathedral
All details as for No. 186, 'Tower of London'.
£125 — £175

No. 192A St. Paul's Cathedral
All details as for No. 190, 'Albert Memorial'.
£40 — £60

No. 193 Charing Cross
One size only and not seen on ware, this lid could only have been produced either during or after 1865, which was the date the 'Eleanor Cross' in the foreground was executed by E.M. Barry. Produced by F. & R. Pratt.
£30 — £50

No. 194 Eleanor Cross
See Nos. 190, 'Albert Memorial', and 192A, 'St. Paul's Cathedral'.

A series of these crosses was originally built by King Edward I, in order to pay homage to his Queen, Eleanor, whose body was brought from Nottinghamshire to Westminster Abbey for burial, and a cross was erected in each place that the cortege rested overnight.
£40 — £60

No. 195 New Houses of Parliament
See No. 186, 'The Tower of London', for details.
£125 — £175

No. 196 The New Blackfriars Bridge
This bridge took four years to build from 1865-69 and, therefore, it is presumed that this lid would originally have been produced c.1870. One size only and not on ware. Produced by F. & R. Pratt.
£25 — £40

No. 197 Thames Embankment
One size only and either with or without title. Produced by F. & R. Pratt. The embankment was constructed between the years 1864-70, which suggests that the date of manufacture was c.1870. Reference to the list of copper plates (Appendix I) will show that two engravings of this subject are contained on the one copper plate (this was for reasons of economy) but the times vary on the clock, which explains the discrepancies which have been remarked on by previous writers. This can be clearly seen on the illustrations shown.
Lids £25 — £40   *Vases £40 — £75*

No. 198 Chapel Royal

These two lids, Nos. 198 and 199, form a pair, and were produced by F. & R. Pratt at the time of the fire, which destroyed a section of the Chapel in 1864. It is recorded that Queen Victoria took an active role in supervising the restoration. Two varieties are known; both lids have a decorative border but others have an extra seaweed border.

Ordinary border . . . . *£30—£50*
Seaweed border . . . . *£50—£75*

No. 199 Choir of Chapel Royal, Savoy

No. 200 Alexandra Palace 1873

Produced by F. & R. Pratt. The date of this lid can, with
certainty, be ascribed to the one shown in the title. In
June 1873 this building was burnt to the ground and was
not re-built until 1875, but the print shows the building
as it was in 1873 before the fire.

Lid only. . . . . *£25—£40*
Complete with base. . *£30—£50*

No. 201 Trafalgar Square

Produced by F. & R. Pratt at the same period as the other London scenes, c.1860-70. The same print was also used
at a later date, c.1880-90, for the vases. These so-called vases are really bottles which contained sauces or relishes.
Either with or without title. Possibly adapted from the painting, 'The Nelson Column', by G. Hawkins (see top
right).

Lids £25 — £40   *Vases £40 — £75*

No. 202 Holborn Viaduct

Produced by F. & R. Pratt. The bridge shown was erected between the years 1867-69, which points to the date of production being contemporary with all the London scenes, c.1870.

£30 — £50

No. 203 New St. Thomas's Hospital

Produced by F. & R. Pratt. As with the previous 'London' lids, the date of production can be confidently given as within a year of the erection of the building in 1870-71.

£30 — £50

A selection of plates which show the range of colours used on tea/dessert wares. The examples shown are from a very large choice of differing colours and borders.

War and Geographical Subjects

No. 204 Golden Horn, Constantinople

Details as for No. 80. The lid was produced in two sizes: the medium size has a fancy chain border, the smaller one is printed to the edge of the lid, with no border. Both this print and No. 80 were registered by J. Ridgway on November 10th, 1854, under the title 'Byzantine'.

Medium size	*£50—£75*
Small size	*£50—£75*

No. 205 The Thirsty Soldier

First issued as 'The Irishman' No. 357, but later adapted to 'The Thirsty Soldier'. Both lids are based on Goodall's painting 'The Tired Soldier' (above right). 'The Irishman' shows a major change by deleting the soldier from the painting and substituting the Irishman. Issued by F. & R. Pratt c.1860-70 in one size only.

£30 — £50

No. 206 Embarking for the East

A scene showing an Highland regiment departing for the Crimea c.1855. Produced by F. & R. Pratt. Two sizes are known, medium and large, the larger size having an extra chain border.

Medium	*£30—£50*
Large	*£40—£60*

No. 207 Washington Crossing the Delaware

A very scarce lid, almost certainly produced by Bates, Walker and Co., 1875-78. Makes a pair with No. 243, and both are similar to the Trentham Hall subjects, Nos. 425 and 426. It may have been produced for the Centenary Celebrations of the American War of Independence.

Large lid	*P.B.N.*
Small lid in monochrome	*P.B.N.*

No. 208 Sebastopol

No. 208A Sebastopol

Produced in two varieties by T.J. & J. Mayer c.1855. No. 208 is in two sizes, the smaller variety having only a line border. The larger size has the spelling Sabastopol instead of Sebastopol. Three soldiers are seen in the foreground, one of whom is mounted. No. 208A is a similar scene with four soldiers in the foreground, two of whom are mounted. Produced on lids only.

Small 208 £50 — £75 *Large 208 £40 — £60* *Medium 208A £40 — £60*

No. 209 Sebastopol
A Pratt lid from the Crimean period, which was also used on dessert plates with various coloured grounds and borders.

Lids	*£50—£75*
Plates according to colour and borders	*£20—£40*

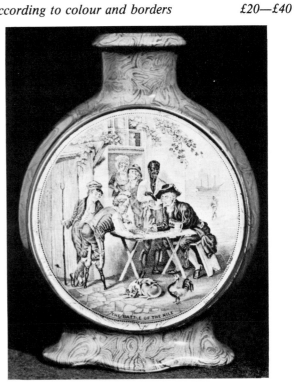

No. 210 The Battle of the Nile
Produced by F. & R. Pratt in one size only, possibly c.1850s. It is difficult to be more precise with this subject which depicts a group discussing Nelson's strategy of the battle fought between the British and French fleets in 1789. Also produced on ware at a much later date, c.1880.

Lids	*£25—£50*
Vases	*£40—£75*

No. 211 Meeting of Garibaldi and Victor Emmanuel

Produced by F. & R. Pratt about 1860-61, the date that Garibaldi accompanied Victor Emmanuel into Naples. Medium size only, but some lids have an extra marbled border.

Medium size	*£25—£40*
Marbled border	*£40—£75*

No. 212 War (after Wouvermann)

A pair of oblong lids by F. & R. Pratt, adapted from the paintings of the celebrated Dutch painter Wouvermann. The signature of J. Austin, as the engraver, is shown on these two lids, with Wouvermann's name shown as the original painter.

Lids only	*£25—£40*
Complete with base	*£30—£50*

No. 213 Peace (after Wouvermann)

No. 214 The Volunteers

No. 215 Old Jack

Produced as a pair, most likely by Bates, Brown-Westhead, Moore and Co., during the period J. Austin was employed there. The volunteers as a force were first enrolled in 1859, and J. Austin was employed by this factory in 1859-60. See also Appendix V. Both lids are in two sizes, small and medium, the medium being larger by the addition of an extra border and produced at a later date.

Either lid with line border   *£60—£80*
Either lid with extra fancy border *£60—£80*

No. 216 The Redoubt

Originally produced by T.J. & J. Mayer as a decorative print on ware such as loving cups, mugs etc., c.1855. Not produced on lids until the copper plates were acquired by Keeling & Co. of Stoke-on-Trent in 1890.

    Lids   *£100—£300*
    Loving cups and mugs   *£150—£250*

No. 217 Conway Castle

All details as for No. 216. Also used on dessert services with a variety of borders. This is one of the lids which needs close scrutiny because production continued up to the 1960s. (See Introduction.)

Lids	*£75—£100*
Plates	*£15—£30*
Comports	*£20—£30*
Late issue lids	*£20—£30*

No. 218 Chin-Chew River

Produced by F. & R. Pratt. Possibly issued c.1860, the date of the war with China. There are several different varieties of this lid; plain double line border, extra seaweed border or extra gold decoration. A series is formed with No. 221 'Harbour of Hong-Kong', No. 222 'Ning Po River' and No. 332 'Transplanting Rice'.

Line border...............	*£25—£40*
Seaweed border...........	*£50—£75*
Complete on decorated pot...	*£75—£100*

No. 219 War

No. 219 War and No. 220 Peace

Produced by F. & R. Pratt. Two lids which have been adapted by J. Austin from the paintings (see illustrations) of Sir Edwin Landseer. Landseer completed them in 1846, and was paid £1,500 for the pair by a Mr. Vernon. First produced 1860-70 and have been reissued many times.

Either lid	*£20—£30*
Marbled pot and lid complete	*£80—£100*

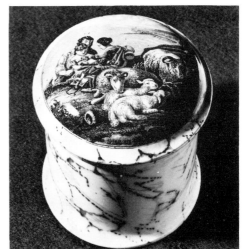

No. 220 Peace

No. 221 Harbour of Hong-Kong

No. 222 Ning Po River

Details as for No. 218, 'Chin-chew River'.
Line border................. £25—£40
Seaweed border.............. £50—£75
Complete on decorated pot..... £75—£100

No. 223 Wimbledon, July 1860

No. 223 Wimbledon, July 1860
No. 224 Rifle Contest, Wimbledon 1864

Two lids produced by F. & R. Pratt as a commemorative of the National Rifle Association, who held their first meeting in 1860. No. 223 shows Queen Victoria firing the first shot on the new range, the rifle being fixed in a vice and trained on to the target. No. 224 (shown opposite), first issued in 1864, was also issued with the date altered to read 1865-1867 and 1868.

Meetings were held at Wimbledon each year until 1889 when the venue was changed to Bisley.

Either lid.................... £25—£40
Marbled surround............. £50—£75
Complete with marbled pot..... £75—£100

No. 224 Rifle Contest, Wimbledon 1864
See caption on page 132.

No. 225 Napirima, Trinidad

No. 225A Napirima, Trinidad
(with advertising)

Two lids, almost certainly produced by T.J. & J. Mayer, c.1853-54. J.S. Fry & Sons, who displayed their goods at the Exhibition in 1851, included views of Napirima, in Trinidad, the growing area of the cocoa-bean, and also of Port of Spain, the principal shipping port. No. 225 is in two sizes, medium and large.

No. 225 Medium £80 — £120   No. 225 Large £80 — £120   No. 225A £250 — £400

Shakespearian Subjects

The following series of Shakespearian subjects on lids and plates were all produced by F. & R. Pratt & Co., at Fenton.

Those with leaf and scroll borders were first issued in the late 1850s. The more common pearl dot border was produced later. Note the spelling of 'Shakspeare' on the lids.

These lids and wares should not be confused with later productions. Messrs. Cauldon Ltd., in the first quarter of this century, issued a series showing these Shakespeare subjects on plates of a finer china body, with a moulded decorative border showing Shakespeare's house and Ann Hathaway's Cottage and the Shakespeare subjects being printed as a centre-piece.

No. 226 Shakespeare's Birthplace (exterior)

Leaf and scroll border	*£80—£120*
Pearl dot border	*£20—£35*
Plates	*£15—£30*

**No. 227 Shakespeare's
Birthplace (interior)**
Leaf and scroll border   £80—£120
Pearl dot border   £20—£35
Plates   £15—£30

**No. 228   Ann Hathaway's
Cottage**
Leaf and scroll border   £80—£120
Pearl dot border   £20—£35
Plates   £15—£30

**No. 229 Holy Trinity Church
Stratford-on-Avon**
Leaf and scroll border £150—£250
Pearl dot border £50—£80
Plates £25—£40

No. 230 Seven Ages of Man
Line border £40—£60
Plates £20—£30

No. 231 Hamlet and His Father's Ghost
Line border £40—£60
Plates £20—£30

Old English Scenes

No. 232 The Village Wakes

A lid produced by F. & R. Pratt in the early 1850s. Several varieties are known: double line border; fancy border; black line and white surround; fancy border on shaped lid and pot (Mr. Fezziwig's Ball); two children, dog and monkey omitted. This is one of the lids which show the name of T. Jackson, who was a manufacturing chemist from Manchester, and a number of lids were registered in his name. Reference to this lid and others bearing Jackson's name, are made elsewhere in this book.

Narrow fancy border.........	*£50—£75*
Fancy border.................	*£60—£80*
Black line and white surround...	*£60—£80*
Fancy border on shaped lid.....	*£70—£100*
Shaped pot and lid complete....	*£100—£150*
With figures deleted..........	*£100—£150*

No. 233 May Day Dancers at the Swan Inn

Almost certainly produced by Bates, Brown-Westhead and Moore c.1860, when Jesse Austin was employed there. The subject is copied from the Le Blond oval of the same name (see above right). Le Blond commenced production of his ovals in 1854 and continued until 1867. Therefore, circumstantial evidence points to Austin using the Le Blond oval as his copy for this lid. Some of the lids are marked S. Banger on the underside. One size only and not seen on ware.

£30 — £50

No. 234 Pet Rabbits

Probably produced by Bates, Brown-Westhead and Moore, based on a Le Blond oval (see above right). The laurel leaf border on this lid is identical to the one used on No. 187 'Strathfieldsay'.

There is certainly more than a thread of coincidence in the details concerning certain of these scarce lids; no actual records are available, no drawings have been seen, no copper plates are in existence, the prints are not seen on any other items and there are no reissues, details which do not apply to lids known to have been produced by either Mayer's or Pratt's. Evidence like this suggests that these lids were produced during the period when Bates was connected with the Cauldon factory, but after he severed connections in 1861, all records appear to have been lost and never recovered.

£500 — £750

No. 235 Il Penseroso

First produced by F. & R. Pratt, possibly in the 1860s, but has been reissued many times. Later issues are very often much paler in colour. One size only and is seen with and without title.

£25 — £40

No. 236 The Parish Beadle

The registration mark, seen at top right, shows this lid to have been registered by Thomas Jackson in 1852 (see No. 232). F. & R. Pratt produced this and the other lids registered by T. Jackson. A very attractive decorative fancy shaped pot and lid was produced, which form a trio with similar shaped pots and covers, No. 232 'The Village Wakes' and No. 238 'Xmas Eve'. Seen with or without title and one size only.

Either with or without title......	*£60—£80*
Shaped lid...................	*£75—£100*
Complete on shaped pot........	*£100—£150*

No. 237 Children of Flora

No definite proof, but almost certainly another product of the Cauldon factory, c.1856-60. Two sizes are known, medium and large. One variety is very attractive, with rim and base colour printed and completed with a gold band round both lid and base. Also seen on ware.

Medium	*£40—£60*
Large	*£40—£60*
Complete with coloured base	*£75—£100*

No. 238 Xmas Eve

Details as for lids No. 232 'The Village Wakes' and No. 236 'The Parish Beadle'. The registration mark, seen at the foot, shows the registration date as 1851. One size only.

Black border or double line	
border	*£60—£80*
Shaped lid	*£75—£100*
Complete with shaped pot	*£100—£150*

The earlier issue of lids with Shakespearian subjects, produced by F. & R. Pratt, the leaf and scroll border being considerably scarcer than the usual line and dot border.

Three unusually large pots and lids by F. & R. Pratt; the only known pots of this diameter, i.e. 7½ins., they are very rare indeed.

No. 239 The Swing

Produced by F. & R. Pratt, c.1860-70, on a variety of items. A very popular subject which was issued over many years. The border of this lid bears a remarkable similarity to the one used on the lids No. 187 'Strathfieldsay' and No. 234 'Pet Rabbits'. One size only.

Lids (early issue)	*£40—£60*
Lids (later issue)	*£20—£40*
Vase	*£100 plus*
Plates according to colour and border	*£15—£30*

No. 240 The Village Wedding

One of the most popular lids issued by F. & R. Pratt, originally c.1857, but reissued many times over the years. This is obvious by the alterations which are observed in the prints; if a lid was very popular and was in demand, it was found necessary to recondition the copper plates, which became worn with excessive use. During such reconditioning, certain items would be altered, for instance on this particular lid the first issue shows a towel lying on the ground, whereas later issues omit this item. Another very important point to look for on the earlier editions of this lid is the registration mark on the jug in the foreground. This shows the design to have been registered by F. & R. Pratt in 1857, but was discontinued in 1883. Lids, therefore, which omit this mark, are almost certainly produced after 1883.

Either with or without towel	£20—£30
Late issues without registration mark	£15—£25
Late issues complete with malachite pot	£25—£40
Late issues complete with gold line pot	£25—£40
Late issues on plates	£15—£20
Late issues on vases	£40—£75

No. 241 Our Home   No. 242 Our Pets

Two lids which form a pair produced for Thomas Jackson by F. & R. Pratt c.1852. The registration marks can be observed at the top right hand (over the woman's head) on 'Our Home' and mid-centre left on 'Our Pets'. One size only, and very often 'Our Pets' is of a paler colour than 'Our Home'. There is in existence a lid of 'Our Home' which has no poetry or title. This is identical to the original drawing of J. Austin and no doubt was an experimental sample lid. Since compiling this book, another lid without poetry or title has been discovered.

Either lid	*£80—£120*
Later issues with white surround	*£75—£100*

Sports and Pastimes

No. 243 The Buffalo Hunt

See No. 207, 'Washington crossing the Delaware'. This large lid 'The Buffalo Hunt' was copied directly from the painting 'An Indian Buffalo Hunt' by George Catlin, an artist responsible for many scenes of American life.

£750 — £1,000

No. 244 The Bull-fight

An early lid by T.J. & J. Mayer, possibly about 1860, which has been reissued many times. One of the lids produced by Kirkhams up to 1960 and, therefore, extreme caution is necessary when acquiring this lid. Several varieties are known.

Medium (no border)............	£100—£150
Large (rosette and dot border).....	£80—£120
Large (marbled border)...........	£100—£150
Tea-pot stands.................	£15—£25
Late issues....................	£10—£30

No. 245 The Enthusiast

One size only and not seen on any other ware. Produced by F. & R. Pratt and first issued c.1860. Reissued many times. From a painting by Lane (see above right):

£25 — £40

No. 246 Blind Man's Buff

Produced by F. & R. Pratt. The design in the candelabra shows this print to have been registered in 1856. Later lids have the registration deleted, also the title. When seen on ware, the title is included, but the candelabra is completely omitted.

With registration mark	*£30—£50*
Without registration mark	*£30—£50*
Shaped mug	*£60—£80*

No. 247 Master of the Hounds

Produced by F. & R. Pratt, a lid in one size only but with several varieties. The common variety has a line border with the title showing at the foot. The rarer varieties have all or any of the following: (a) no title, (b) gold rim, (c) screwtop, (d) workman's mark on the reverse. Particular attention should be paid to colour with this lid; many late varieties are seen with very pale colours. Probably first issued c.1855-60 and was adapted by J. Austin from the painting 'Drawn Blank'.

Line border	*£30—£50*
Late issues	*£15—£30*
Rare varieties	*£200 plus*

No. 248 Chiefs Return from Deer-stalking

Produced by F. & R. Pratt. No early issues of this lid have been seen. Details are given in the Introduction of the significance of different crazing allied to the date of production. This is very obvious with this particular lid. The crazing is the large type so well-known with lids produced c.1800-90, and the lid is rather heavier in texture than is usual. This lid was produced contemporary with late issues of No. 174 'The Blue Boy'. Reference to the existing list of copper plates (Appendix I) shows them to have been produced simultaneously from one copper plate.

£50 — £80

No. 249 Dangerous Skating
Produced by F. & R. Pratt, two varieties of this lid are known; one shows five steps, the other has six steps, first issued c.1850. One size only and was also used on ware. A later issue has an extra fancy border. One of the prints was reissued in Holland c.1850-60, with the title engraved in Dutch.

Either variety	£25—£40
Plates	£15—£25

No. 250 Fair Sportswoman
Produced by Bates, Brown-Westhead and Moore at Cauldon, c.1860, in two sizes, medium and large. Varieties are known with coloured bases and lids which usually have a gold rim. Dessert plates are seen with this print (see page 149, top right), and a trio is formed with No. 337 'The Flute Player' and No. 431 'The Spanish Dancers'.

No border	£30—£50
Coloured base and lid complete	£75—£100
Plates	£20—£30

148

No. 250 Fair Sportswoman
See caption on page 148

No. 251 A False Move

First issued by T.J. & J. Mayer c.1850, this lid depicts a political cartoon of the time, relating to a letter issued by Cardinal Wiseman to the Catholic churches, which received adverse comment from the Protestants. In view of the general outcry, Cardinal Wiseman had to withdraw his remarks and state that the letter was meant only for the Catholics.

Two sizes are known, medium and large. The large size has a decorative border with the title at the foot and the medium size has no border and no title. Great caution is necessary with this subject; there have been many reissues, and it is included in the list of lids produced up to 1960 by Kirkhams (Appendix III).

Large size	*£120—£150*
Medium size	*£150—£200*
Reissues	*£20—£30*

No. 252 A Pair
A Pratt lid only produced in one size, c.1860, but reissued many times over the years. Unusual but not unknown on ware.

Lids	*£20—£30*
Mugs	*£30—£50*

No. 253 Snap-dragon

Several varieties of this lid by F. & R. Pratt are known, either with or without title, and the moon showing through the window. The mark, which shows the date of registration as August 9th 1856, is usually missing on items of ware. This points to a date of manufacture possibly after 1883 when this particular mark ceased to be used. Possibly copied from 'The Snap-dragon Polka', the cover of which is shown.

Lids (either variety).... £40—£60
Plates............... £15—£30
Mugs .... £60—£80

No. 254 The Best Card

Produced by F. & R. Pratt, c.1860-70. Two varieties are known, the later issue having an extra decorative fancy brown border.

Either variety £25 — £40

No. 255 Hide and Seek

Produced by F. & R. Pratt, c.1860-70. One size only, a very popular lid produced over many years, based on the painting by T.A. Ross (above right).

£20 — £30

No. 256 A Fix

This particular lid was produced by T.J. & J. Mayer and by F. & R. Pratt. The Mayer lid (see above) does not show the barrel and broom seen in Pratt's issue (see below). Both firms concerned issued more than one variety. Pratt's have the early issue with line border, the later issue having a decorative fancy border. Mayer's have the early issue with no border, the later issue having a white surround.

Line border	*£30—£50*	*No border*	*£50—£75*
Fancy border	*£40—£60*	*White surround*	*£40—£60*

153

No. 257 A Race *or* Derby Day

Medium size only and not seen on ware. Produced over many years by F. & R. Pratt.

£25 — £40

No. 258 The Skaters

One size only and no border. Produced by F. & R. Pratt, c.1860-70. Not seen on ware.

£30 — £50

No. 259 The Sportsman

Manufactured by F. & R. Pratt, c.1860-70. Two varieties are known, either with or without the title. Produced at a later date on items of ware.

With title........	£25—£40
Without title.....	£25—£40
Vase	£40—£75

No. 260 The Game Bag

Produced by F. & R. Pratt, c.1860-70, either with or without title, and one size only. Also produced at a later date on ware. Lee's painting 'The cover side' is shown below right.

With title .... *£25—£40*
Without title ..... *£25—£40*
Vase .... *£40—£75*

No. 261 Pheasant Shooting

T.J. & J. Mayer first issued this lid c.1855-60, but the print was used over a fairly long period and ware has been seen with the date 1868. The original issues of this lid are extremely scarce, but it is necessary to use extreme caution when buying this lid, as it was reissued by Kirkhams and has been seen completely moulded to include a black framed surround. Two sizes are known, medium and large.

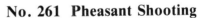

Early issues, line border	*£100—£125*
Early issues, marbled border	*£125—£150*
Jug	*£75—£100*
Reissues	*£20—£30*
Mugs	*£50—£80*

No. 262 The Boar Hunt

Produced by T.J. & J. Mayer, c.1855-60, in two sizes, and like the previous lid, was reissued by Kirkhams up to the 1960s. Great care is required with this lid. The original issue in a medium size is an extremely scarce lid. Also produced in a larger size with a decorative border.

Medium size	*£200—£300*
Large size	*£150—£250*
Reissues	*£20—£30*
Tea-pot stands	*£20—£30*

No. 263 Children Sailing Boats in Tub

A lid from F. & R. Pratt, used not only on lids, but also on ware. Based on the painting 'Contrary Winds' (see right). One size only with line and dotted border.

Lids	*£30—£50*
Mugs	*£60—£80*

Dogs and other Animals

No. 264 Dogs

A series of dog subjects by F. & R. Pratt, which can be seen on a variety of items: lids, jugs, two-handled loving cups, etc. The ware usually has very attractive ground-laid colourings in blue, pink, maroon or black. Rather later in period than the usual range, these lids and ware are dated approximately 1870-80. All these subjects are copied from various paintings of Sir Edwin Landseer. A print based on one of these paintings is shown below.

Coalport have recently produced a pair of vases from the original copper plates, showing six dogs and nine dogs respectively. These can be seen on pages 159 and 161.

The lids are numbered from 264(a) to 264(f) according to the number of dogs shown, which vary from four to nine. There are three varieties known of 264(c) Six Dogs, and two varieties of 264(f) Nine Dogs.

Pot-lids £100 — £200   *Jugs £150+*   *Mugs £150+*

264(a) Four Dogs

264(c) Six Dogs

264(c)   Six Dogs (variety)

264(d)   Seven Dogs

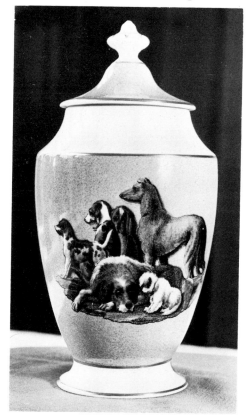

264(c)   Six Dogs (variety)

Unusual shapes and colourings on pots and lids from both F. & R. Pratt and T.J. & J. Mayer. The tall pots were made to contain powders and a powder puff.

Items which were produced on utilitarian wares, such as butter dishes, cream jugs, sugar basins, flasks, powder bowls, etc. Produced by F. & R. Pratt c.1890-1920, but using the early original copper plates to decorate the wares.

264(e) Eight Dogs

264(f) Nine Dogs

No. 265 Good Dog

A large lid, one size only, from the factory of F. & R. Pratt, c.1870. The title of this lid can be seen on the rock in the foreground. As with the majority of these prints showing dogs, Landseer was the artist responsible for the drawing (above right) which J. Austin adapted for his engraving. Dessert ware was produced showing this print, probably up to as late as 1890-1900.

Lids	*£30—£50*
Plates	*£20—£30*

No. 266 Contrast

A Pratt lid produced c.1865, adapted by Austin from Landseer's 'Dogs'. Dessert ware with this print was also produced at a later date than the lids.

Lids	*£30—£50*
Plates	*£15—£30*

No. 267 Feeding the Chickens

An early lid, probably from Bates, Brown-Westhead & Moore, c.1860. Some of the lids are marked with the name S. Banger on the underside. One size only and not seen on ware.

£30 — £50

No. 268 A Gay Dog

One of the few lids which are very difficult to attribute to a particular factory. The similarity of this lid with Nos. 7-11 and 12 leads one to assume that it was produced by J. Ridgway & Co. at Cauldon in the early 1850s. The usual pattern is so apparent — no records, not seen on ware, very rare etc., all pointers which apply to the very early lids from J. Ridgway.

£250 — £500

No. 269 Deerhound Guarding Cradle

Produced by F. & R. Pratt between 1860-90. Several varieties are known: flat top with seaweed decoration, domed top with marbled decoration, or plain line and dot border. The ware seen was produced later than the lids. The deerhound shown in the print was taken from Landseer's 'High Life'.

Flat top with seaweed decoration	£40—£60
Flat top with seaweed decoration complete on tall pot	£80—£100
Domed top with marbled decoration	£40—£60
Line and dot border	£30—£40
Plate	£15—£30
Mug	£30—£50

No. 270 The Begging Dog

Produced by F. & R. Pratt between 1860-90. One size only and later used on ware. Another lid adapted by J. Austin from Landseer's paintings of dogs; in this instance it is from the painting entitled 'The Beggar' (see above left).

Lids	*£30—£50*
Mugs	*£60—£80*

No. 271 Pompey and Caesar
All details as for lid No. 270, except that J. Austin used Landseer's painting 'The Cavalier's Pets' for his design (see above right).

Lids	*£100—£125*
Mugs	*£60—£80*

No. 272 Both Alike

Details as for lid No. 270, except that J. Austin used a composite picture, by copying the dogs from Landseer's painting 'The Breakfast Party', which is shown above left.

£25 — £40

No. 273 Country Quarters

Produced by F. & R. Pratt in one size only between 1860-90. Not yet seen on ware.

£30 — £50

No. 274 High Life

Two lids produced by F. & R. Pratt between 1860-90 as a pair. Copied directly from Landseer's paintings of the same name (shown for reference).

Either lid £25 — £40

No. 275 Low Life

No. 276 The Snow-drift

Produced by F. & R. Pratt, 1860-90. May be seen either with or without title. Again, a copy of one of Landseer's paintings — 'Highland Shepherd's Dog in the Snow', often referred to erroneously as 'The Rescue' or 'The Snow-drift' (above right).

Either with or without title £25 — £40

No. 277 The Skewbald Horse. See caption page 170.

No. 277 The Skewbald Horse

Produced by F. & R. Pratt, 1860-90. A popular subject reissued over a number of years on wares of varied design. The lid shows not only the name of P. Wouvermann, from whose painting the engraving was copied by J. Austin, but also Austin's name as the engraver. These details were included in each issue until the death of Austin in 1879, after which reissues omitted his name. Two varieties of the lid are known, one with a narrow fancy border and one with seaweed decoration.

Narrow border	*£30—£50*
Seaweed border	*£40—£60*
Seaweed border complete on pot	*£75—£100*
Plates	*£15—£30*
Pilgrim shape vase	*£40—£75*
Vases	*£100 plus*

Birds

The items in the following series are quite scarce, and mainly only found on ware. Wherever lids are known, they will be mentioned, all such lids being very late in period, possibly between 1890-1920. Plates have a variety of ground-laid colours, particularly greens, reds and blues. In addition to the items mentioned, bird subjects will be found on a variety of items such as mugs, cups and saucers, jugs etc., when prices must be at the discretion of the purchaser. Nos. 278-294 were produced by Pratt between 1860 and 1890.

No. 278 The Robin

Plate £80 — £120   *Jug £80 — £120*   *Coalport reissue plates £60*

No. 279 A Pair of Wrens
Plate £80 — £120   Lids £30 — £50
Coalport reissue plates £60

No. 280 The Goldfinch
Plate £80 — £120

No. 281 The Cuckoo
Plate £80 — £120

No. 282 Blue Tit and Long-tailed Tit

Plate	*£80—£120*
Lids	*£30—£50*
Vase	*£100—£200*
Coalport reissue plate	*£60*

No. 283 The Swallow
Plate £80 — £120

No. 284 The Bullfinch and the Canary
Plate £80 — £120   Lids £30 — £50

No. 285 The Reed Warbler
Plate £80 — £120   Lids £30 — £50
Coalport reissue plate £60

Birds

No. 286 Snowy Owl and Young
Plate £80 — £120   Jug £80 — £120
Coalport reissue plate £60

No. 287 The Kestrel
Plate £80 — £120   Lids £30 — £50

No. 288 The Buzzard
Plate £80 — £120   Lids £30 — £50

No. 289 The Sea Eagle
Plate £80 — £120   Lids £30 — £50

No. 290 The Condor and The Snake
Plate £80 — £120

No. 291 The Heron
Bowl £80 — £120   Coalport reissue plate £60

No. 292 Eagle Owl and Merlin
Coalport reissue plate £60

No. 293 The Thrush

Plate	£80—£120
Vase	£100—£200
Lids	£30—£50
Coalport reissue plate	£60

These colourful and decorative plates are extremely desirable. The full service would consist of twelve plates, each with a different bird subject, and six comports. Very scarce and priced accordingly. Produced by F. & R. Pratt.

No. 294 The Chaffinch
Also known on other items of ware.
Dish £50 — £80

No. 295A The Nightingale

No. 295B The Skylark

Two plates manufactured by Wood and Baggaley c.1870-80. These plates are included as further examples of underglaze colour printing, but the quality does not compare with that of either Mayer or Pratt. Marked on reverse as shown.

Either plate £25 — £40

No. 296 The Kingfisher

T.J. & J. Mayer originally issued this lid c.1850. Later issues of this lid, with plates and teapot stands were produced by Bates, Elliott and Co., c.1870.

Early lids	*P.B.N.*	*Plates*	*£80—£120*
Late issue lids	*£20—£30*	*Teapot stands*	*£25—£40*

No. 267 The Swallow. See caption on page 180.

No. 297 The Swallow

Issued by Bates, Elliott & Co., in December 1870 (registration on underside, as shown). Two sizes are known; the smaller size lacks some of the foliage seen on the larger lid. Plates and jugs have been seen with this print and border. A variation shows plates with 'branches and leaves' replacing the floral border.

Medium size............................ £80—£120
Small size............................. £80—£120
Plates................................. £30—£50
Jugs................................... £30—£50
Later issue without registration mark...... £50—£75

All the following items, shown on pages 181-183, are from the Pratt factory and usually only seen on ware, cups, jugs, mugs, etc.

No. 298 The Bullfinch

Mugs .... £50—£100
Cups .... £40—£60
Cups with saucer .... £80—£100
Jugs .... £80—£100
Plates .... £50—£80
Tea kettle .... £100—£150
    Other items priced according to circumstances

No. 299 Yellow Hammer

No. 300 Nightingale

No. 301 The Goldfinch

No. 302 The Wren

No. 303 The Blue Tit

No. 304 The Storm Petrel

No. 305 Red-backed Shrike

No. 306 Lesser-spotted Woodpecker

No. 307 The Owl

Pictorial, Landscape and General Subjects

No. 308 Dutch Winter Scene

A small lid first issued by F. & R. Pratt c.1860. A popular subject which was also in use for many years on items of ware produced up to and including the 1890s.

Lids . . . . £30—£50
Plates . . . . . . £15—£30
Mugs . . . . £60—£80

No. 309 The Faithful Shepherd
(see opposite)

No. 309 The Faithful Shepherd

Details as for No. 308, with the addition of several different varieties of the lid. The borders vary, line and dotted border, marbled border, seaweed border, and highly domed top with marbled border. Dessert ware was also produced later in the period.

Copied from a painting by Nicholas Berghem (1624-83), a Dutch painter. 'Berghem' means 'hide him' in Dutch. The name was apparently given to Berghem by his fellow pupils after an incident in which his tutor was hiding him from his father.

$$\begin{array}{ll} \textit{Line border....} & \textit{£30—£50} \\ \textit{Marbled border} & \textit{£50—£75} \\ \textit{Seaweed border} & \textit{£50—£75} \\ \textit{Plates........} & \textit{£15—£30} \end{array}$$

No. 310 H.R.H. Prince of Wales visiting the Tomb of Washington

Produced by F. & R. Pratt, c.1861, to commemorate the Prince of Wales's visit to the United States and Canada in 1860. One size only and is not seen on ware.

£30 — £50

185

No. 311 I See You, My Boy

Produced at the Pratt factory in the 1860s. A very popular print which was used on both lids and ware. Two varieties are known: one has a boy with a blue cap, the other has a boy with a red cap. Both varieties are signed 'J.A.' on the lower left, and have the title at the foot, within the print.

This print was also used on a tall marbled pot with a high domed top, which may have the words 'J. Gosnell & Co., London', within a scroll on the base. One of the products of this firm was 'Toilet Powder' and containers so marked usually have a scroll displayed with the wording:

"Calcutta Medical College, 23rd July 1880.
I have examined Chemically and Microscopically the contents of a packet of Toilet & Nursery Powder prepared by John Gosnell & Co., London, and find that it consists of perfumed starch, and is free from all admixture of injurious mineral or vegetable matter.
C.J.H. Warden
Chemical examiner to Government.''

Lids	*£20—£30*
Domed lid and base	*£80—£120*
Plates	*£15—£30*
Pilgrim vase	*£40—£75*
Triangular vase with mauve and green scroll decoration	*P.B.N.*

No. 311 I See You, My Boy
(see opposite)

No. 312 French Street Scene
Issued by F. & R. Pratt in two sizes for Messrs. Crosse
and Blackwell. The print shows a street in Strasbourg
and the contents of the pot were probably 'Strasbourg
paste', a delicacy being produced by Crosse and
Blackwell c.1860-70.

Medium size	*£25—£40*	
Large size	*£25—£40*	

No. 313 Cottage Children

A large lid, the subject of which was adapted by Austin for F. & R. Pratt from Gainsborough's painting of the same title (see illustration). First issued c.1850-60 with many later editions, which were produced up to the 1890s. A vase, recently discovered, is shown on page 287.

Fancy border	£100—£200
Malachite border (Plaque) ...	£100—£200
Plates....................	£20—£40
Late issues................	£20—£30

No. 314 The Breakfast Party

T.J. & J. Mayer produced this lid c.1850, and no late issues are known, neither is it seen on ware. Produced in two sizes, medium and large, and usually with marbled border.

Any variety £75 — £100

No. 315 Cattle and Ruins

Issued over many years by F. & R. Pratt, originally produced c.1860. Two sizes are known, medium and large, the larger one having an extra fancy border, with an additional variety having seaweed decoration on both lid and base. Considerable use was made of this print, not only on lids but quite extensively on dessert ware, in conjunction with varied decorative borders and ground-laid colours.

Medium or large lid.............. £25—£40
Seaweed rim complete with base... £75—£100
Plates .... £15—£30
Vases......................... £50—£100

316 Lady, Boy and Goats

Similar period as No. 315, also from F. & R. Pratt. Only produced in one size, and again used on ware but not so popular as 'Cattle and Ruins'. One of the many designs by J. Austin and based on a painting by Landseer, 'Harvest-time in the Scottish Highlands' (see below).

Lids	*£40—£75*
Mugs	*£60—£80*

No. 317 Lend a Bite

Another painting copied by J. Austin for F. & R. Pratt, c.1860, in this instance from one by Mulready entitled 'Lending a bite' (shown for comparison).

The vase appears to be very attractively printed in imitation marbling but this was easily achieved by an incomplete process. These containers for sauces were produced c.1890, and the process of decoration gave the very poor imitation of the excellent malachite printing of the 1850s. This was achieved by first printing in blue/grey marbling and completed by hand-colouring in a green wash colour which, when fired, gave the rather poor results seen on the completed item. The one illustrated has probably not been completed with the green colour, confirmed by the lack of gold line decoration, which is seen on the majority of these containers.

Lids	*£25—£40*
Vases	*£40—£75*

No. 318 The Old Water-mill

Produced by F. & R. Pratt, in one size only, c.1860. Several varieties are known: line and dot border, seaweed decorated border, and on a shaped pot with either of the borders mentioned. Another subject copied from a painting 'Travellers Conversing', by Nicholas Berghem (see No. 309).

Line and dot border . . . . £40—£60
Seaweed border . . . . £50—£75
Complete on shaped pot . . . . . £75—£120

No. 319 The Queen, God Bless Her
(see opposite)

No. 319 The Queen, God Bless Her

A print produced at the Pratt factory about 1860, but was continually in demand for many years. This is evident by the number of items bearing this print and the slight differences which were the result of worn copper plates being reconditioned. For instance, early examples show the title, as above, within the print, whereas later examples have no title showing.

Single decorative border without title . . . . £25—£40	*Seaweed border and complete on pot* . . . . £75—£100
Single decorative border with title . . . . £25—£40	*Plates* . . . . £15—£30
Double decorative border without title . . . . . . £25—£50	*Vases* . . . . £100 plus
Double decorative border with title . . . . £25—£50	*Teapot stands* . . . . £25—£40

No. 320 Mother and Daughters

A rare lid known to be in two sizes, the origin of which is not known. It is an early lid c.1850 and could possibly have been produced by J. Ridgway and Co., at Cauldon, but there is no definite supporting evidence. There are differing varieties; the lady's hair is either black or red, the borders can vary with the number of lines, some lids have a gold band, others are coloured pink and others have a pink surround plus a gold band. Unrecorded on ware.

Either size................... £100—£200
Gold band.................. £150—£250
Pink surround complete on pot.. £150—£300

No. 321 Deer Drinking

A popular subject produced over many years from the Pratt factory, first issued c.1860. Only in one size, with either plain rim or seaweed decorative rim and pot. Also used on dessert ware. J. Austin's drawing (see p.195, top left) shows the differences often made between drawing and engraving. A rabbit in the foreground was omitted from the engraving.

Plain variety......................... £25—£40
Seaweed variety complete with pot ...... £75—£100
Plates .... £15—£30

No. 321 Deer Drinking
J. Austin's drawing for 'Deering Drinking'
See page 194

No. 322 The Rivals
First issued by F. & R. Pratt c.1860. Only one size known and was in production for a number of years. Not usually seen on ware.

Lid	*£30—£50*
Marbled border	*£50—£75*

No. 323 The Dentist
One size only, first issued by F. & R. Pratt c.1850-60 and reissued many times since that date. Most lids now seen are of the late variety, c.1880. From a painting by Isach Van Ostade (above right).

Early issue	*£50—£100*
Early (screw-top)	*£100—£200*
Late issue	*£30—£50*

A mixture of items used on the tea table. Various shaped cups, saucers, tea-pots, sugar basins, jugs, etc., in a variety of colours, are to be found.

No. 324 The Farriers

From F. & R. Pratt c.1860, one of the lids which has both the signature of the artist, Wouvermann, and the engraver J. Austin. A large size lid, not usually seen on ware.

£30 — £50

No. 325 The Shepherdess

No. 326 The Shepherd Boy

Both lids were produced by the Cauldon factory, c.1855-65, possibly during the period when J. Austin was employed at that factory by Bates, Brown-Westhead and Moore and Co. Very popular subjects, which were produced in two sizes, medium and large, and with a number of variations in decoration. Lids and bases are known with maroon or green ground-laid colours, others with extra gold lines on both lid and base.

Either medium or large	*£30—£50*
Ground-laid coloured bases and lids complete	*£50—£75*
Extra gold lines, bases and lids complete	*£50—£75*
Very late issues with large white border	*£20—£30*

No. 327 The Times
Copied by J. Austin from the painting, 'The Newspaper' by T.S. Goode (above right), for F. & R. Pratt, c.1860-70. One size only, with the title showing at the foot.

£20 — £40

No. 328 Uncle Toby
One of the most popular lids by F. & R. Pratt, c.1860-70. Reissued many times over the years to 1890, with differences in colour in Uncle Toby's coat, which can either be red or purple. An engraving copied by J. Austin from C.R. Leslie's painting (above right) depicting an incident from Laurence Sterne's noval *Tristram Shandy*. Incidentally, the widow's efforts did bear fruit; she eventually got Uncle Toby to marry her.

£20 — £30

No. 329a

No. 329b

No. 329c

No. 329c

No. 329 The First Appeal

Originally issued by F. & R. Pratt c.1855, with further issues possibly to c.1890.

No. 329a, the first issue, is in two sizes and has no wording or lettering round the rim, except for the title seen at the foot. Examples are also known without the title.

No. 329b, the second issue, is also in two sizes, but there are several alterations. The door in the first issue is replaced by a window, the trees are replaced by a door, and the girl who is looking down in the first issue, is now looking up.

No. 329c, the third issue, again shows alterations; the girl now has no cap, her hair is shortened, and she is wearing a dress with red and white strips. The wording — 'I consent', she replied, ' if you promise that no jealous rival shall laugh me to scorn' — is seen round both prints No. 329b and No. 329c.

Two sizes are known. Also seen on ware.

First issue	£150—£250	*Plates*	£15—£30
Second issue	£40—£60	*Vases*	£100 plus
Third issue	£25—£40		

No. 330a

No. 330b

No. 330 The Second Appeal

Details as No. 329, with which it is paired. Two issues are known of this lid. The first issue (No. 330a) is extremely scarce and has no wording or lettering.

The second issue (No. 330b) shows a number of differences; the well, bucket and pitcher shown on the first issue, are deleted, and are replaced by a large stone, on which stands a basket. The man wears a hat and has boots, whilst the girl, not only now has a hat, she also wears a red striped dress, instead of a coat and skirt, as in the first issue. Two varieties are known of this second issue, which is in two sizes, medium and large. One shows the girl with the red striped dress, whilst the other has no stripes showing, and has the addition of a gold band. Both lids have, round the edge, the wording 'No: by heaven I exclaimed may I perish if ever I plant in that bosom a thorn'.

First issue................ P.B.N.
Either variety second issue... £25—£40
Plates.................... £15—£30

No. 331 Strasburg

Produced by T.J. & J. Mayer, c.1850-55. A very popular lid, which usually has a grey and white marbled rim and base, and occasionally is seen with extra gold lines. Produced by Mayer's for Crosse and Blackwell, who used it for their product, 'Strasburg paste'. Two sizes are known, medium and large.

Either size................ £25—£40
Complete on marbled base... £30—£50

200

No. 332 Transplanting Rice

By F. & R. Pratt c.1860. See No. 218 for details.

Line border . . . . *£25—£40*
Seaweed border . . . . *£50—£75*
Complete on decorated pot . . . *£75—£100*

No. 333   Vue de la Ville de Strasbourg
Prise du Port

Produced in two sizes, medium and large, by F. & R. Pratt, c.1855-60, for Messrs. Crosse and Blackwell. A popular print, used over many years and reissued on dessert ware, c.1870-80.

Either size   *£30—£50*
Plates   *£15—£30*

No. 334 The Trooper

Copied by J. Austin for F. & R. Pratt, c.1860-70, from a composite picture (see Appendix IV). Many late issues of this lid are seen, and it was also used on dessert ware, possibly up to 1890, usually poorer colours than the earlier issues. Medium size only, and a pair with No. 356, 'The Cavalier'.

Lids	£25—£40
Plates	£15—£30
Vases	£40—£75

No. 335 Fording the Stream

Medium size only. Produced by F. & R. Pratt, c.1860-65. The earlier variety has the signature J.A. on the stone at the lower right-hand size, but this is omitted on later varieties.

Either variety	£25—£40
Vase	£40—£75

No. 336a Street Scene on the Continent

No. 336b Street Scene on the Continent

Presumed to have been produced by F. & R. Pratt, due to the similarity of this lid and base with others known to have been produced by Pratt's.

No. 336a is usually seen in two colours, either green or red ground-laid colours, with a fancy scroll border on both lid and base.

No. 336b is usually in green only, with the border of No. 123 on both lid and base. The figures in No. 336a are omitted, and the stone bridge is replaced by a pole and chain bridge.

Either variety, lids only   *£30—£50*
Either variety, complete with pot   *£50—£80*

No. 337 The Flute Player

All details as No. 250, 'Fair Sportswoman'.

Either size — print vignetted. . . . . .   *£30—£50*
Coloured lid and base complete. . . .   *£50—£75*
Plates . . . .   *£15—£30*

No. 338 Grace before Meals

An early lid by F. & R. Pratt, c.1850. Two examples of this lid are known to have dates inscribed in gold on the underside. One of these examples is very lavishly decorated with a raised border in gold, with gold lines and gold flecked marbling as extra decoration, with the date December 31st 1847. This may have been the date of production, but it is more likely to have been a personal commemorative date. The other example is not so decorative, and has no raised border, with the date D.C. 1850. This is probably someone's initials, and the date commemorative of that person. The original painting by Jan Steen is shown above right.

White surround . . . . £80—£120
Marbled surround . . . . £125—£175
With date 1850 . . . . £150—£200
Complete with gold flecked pot and
dated 1847 . . . . P.B.N.
Plates . . . . £15—£30

No. 339 The Vine Girl

The registration mark (above left) on the underside shows this print to have been registered by Bates, Elliot and Co., on June 1st, 1874. Produced in two sizes, medium and large, and also seen without the registration mark, probably a later issue.

Either size....... *£40—£80*
Plates........... *£15—£30*
Teapot stands.... *£20—£30*

No. 340 On Guard

A lid in medium size only, produced by F. & R. Pratt, c.1860, but many later issues are seen. Two varieties are known; the earlier issue shows a bucket under the seat, and the later one shows the bucket replaced by a dog.
Either variety £20 — £30

No. 341 The Fisher-boy

A small lid, in the one size only, produced by F. & R. Pratt during a period extending from approximately 1860-90. Based on the painting, 'The Fisher-boy', by J.G. Naish (see below).

Lids £30 — £50   Mugs £60 — £80

No. 342a Summer

Three subjects registered on June 1st, 1874, by Bates, Elliott and Co. (see mark shown above). Earlier issues of 342a and 342b have the registration mark on the underside. 342c is only seen on plaques, and forms a pair with 342a, which is also known on a plaque.

Lids with registration . . . .   *£60—£80*
Lids without registration . . . .   *£30—£50*
Single plaques . . . .   *£75—£100*
Pair plaques . . . . *£200—£250*

No. 342b Autumn

No. 342c Spring

No. 343 The Maidservant
Not seen on ware. Produced by F. & R. Pratt c.1860, in one size only.

£60 — £80
Complete on shaped pot £100 — £125

No. 344 Negro and Pitcher
A large lid by F. & R. Pratt, of which no early issues are known. Several similar late issues are known, such as No. 364, 'The Strawberry Girl', No. 217, 'Conway Castle', No. 352, 'The Quarry', etc. The probable date of production is approximately 1880-85, and details have been given in the Introduction concerning these later lids, namely that 'much heavier texture and larger crazing are invariably signs of a later issue'. Very occasionally seen on dessert plates.

Lids £80 — £125   *Plates £30 — £50*

No. 345 Girl with Grapes

Made for J. Gosnell and Co., by F. & R. Pratt, over
several years, with the first issue c.1850-60. Several
varieties are known; with the print to the edge of the lid,
with plain line border, line and dot border, marbled
border with dome top lid. Screw top lids are also
known. J. Austin copied a painting by Murillo, whose
name is seen at the foot of the lid.

Any variety as above.................	*£25—£40*
Marbled border.....................	*£50—£75*
Marbled border complete on marbled pot	*£75—£100*
Screw top lid.......................	*£100—£200*

No. 346 Tam-o-Shanter and Souter Johnny

Two lids, Nos. 346 and 347, from the Cauldon factory, when owned by Bates, Brown-Westhead and Moore & Co., c.1860, produced in two sizes, medium and large. The creamy fawn colouring of these lids is peculiar to Cauldon and is not seen on lids from any other factory. Ware is seen, produced at a later date, but the creamy texture is not observed with these later items. The drawing of Tam-o-Shanter by Thomas is shown below left.

Either size	*£50—£75*
Teapot stands	*£20—£30*

No. 347 Tam-o-Shanter

No. 348 Peasant Boys

There are many varieties of this lid produced by F. & R. Pratt, c.1850-60, for J. Gosnell and Co., in one size only. Issues are shown larger, by the addition of extra borders.

There are several varieties: (a) line and narrow fancy border with white surround; (b) with gold line and narrow gold flecked marbled pot; (c) with gold line only (no fancy border) on slightly taller gold flecked marbled pot; (d) with seaweed border on taller pot; (e) dome top on tall marbled pot complete.

A print from Murillo's painting, 'Spanish Beggar-boys', is shown below.

(a) Line and fancy border	*£25—£40*
(b) Gold flecked pot complete 1^{1}/$_{10}$ins. deep	*£40—£60*
(c) Gold flecked pot complete and gold line 1¾ins. deep	*£40—£60*
(d) Seaweed border complete on pot 2¼ins. deep	*£60—£80*
(e) Marbled dome top complete on pot 3½ins. deep	*£80—£120*
Vases	*£100 plus*

Lids priced as complete on matching pots, adjustments to be made for lids only.

No. 349 The Poultry Woman

Another lid from the Pratt factory, possibly first produced in the 1860s and for many years thereafter. The early editions of this print show the initials J.A. on the right lower edge and Jesse Austin's original drawing is still in existence. Tea plates are seen with various coloured grounds, such as pink or red, but the most attractive pieces of ware with this print are the triangular shaped vases similar to No. 58, 'The Fishbarrow' and No. 311, 'I see you, my boy'.

Lids . . . .   *£25—£40*
Plates . . . .   *£15—£30*
Triangular vase with gold and blue decoration . . . .   *P.B.N.*
Triangular vase with mauve and green scroll decoration . . . . .   *P.B.N.*
Triangular vase in white with Soyer portrait . . . .   *£150—£200*

Part of a malachite dessert service. The full service, consisting of eighteen pieces, makes a very impressive display. The 1851 Exhibition was the venue chosen to introduce this excellent service.

A very desirable tea/coffee service manufactured by F. & R. Pratt, again rather late in period, c.1890, but using the original copper plates for the decoration.

No. 350 Halt by the Wayside

This is on one of the copper plates which contain four engravings, in this case No. 54 'Examining the Nets', No. 350 'Halt by the Wayside', No. 443 'The Milkmaid', No. 445 'The Stall-woman', but only one of these has yet been seen on lids, No. 54 'Examining the Nets'. Possibly, this situation is explained by the fact that No. 54, 'Examining the Nets', is also preserved on a separate copper plate, with one important difference, the composite copper plate (as mentioned above) carries an extra green colour, whereas the single copper plate used for the lid, only has four colours (see Appendix I).

Cups . . . . . £25—£35
Plates . . . . £25—£35
Saucers . . . £25—£35
Tiles . . . . . £25—£35

WITHDRAWN-UNL

No. 351 Preparing for the Ride

From F. & R. Pratt c.1860, produced over many years. Medium size only, but two varieties are known; the plume in the hat on the ground can be either blue or red and the horse can be dappled or grey. A popular subject, also used on dessert ware. A print from the painting 'Preparing for the chase' by Mourenhout is shown right.

Either variety	*£30—£50*
Plates	*£15—£30*

No. 352 The Quarry

Details as for No. 344, 'Negro and Pitcher'. Reference to the list of drawings shows this subject to have been copied by J. Austin from a Wouvermann painting entitled 'Landscape' (for comparison, see left). Has been seen on tiles produced at the same period.

Lids	*£80—£125*
Tiles	*£50—£80*

No. 353 Persuasion

Medium size only, by F. & R. Pratt, c.1860, but produced both on lids and dessert plates over many years. The later issues of this lid are very often seen with poorer colours.

Lids	£30—£50
Plates	£15—£30
Vases	£40—£75

No. 354 The Picnic

A large lid produced c.1860 by F. & R. Pratt. Only the one variety known.

£30 — £50

No. 355a Royal Coat of Arms

No. 355b Royal Coat of Arms

One size only but with two varieties; on one the name J.N. Osborn is seen on the scroll below the coat of arms and on the other the scroll is blank. This is one of the few lids whose factory of origin is unknown.

  J.N. Osborn was a member of a family who specialised in manufacturing and selling anchovy paste during the latter half of the 19th century. Lids have been seen with the wording 'Thornes inimitable potted bloater, anchovy and preserved meats, No. 82 York Road, Lambeth' round the border.

  (a)   With name   £125—£250
  (b)   Without name   £125—£250

No. 356 The Cavalier

Details as for No. 334, 'The Trooper', with which it forms a pair. Originally issued by F. & R. Pratt c.1860, but produced over many years on different items of ware. The later issues of the lid often have poorer colours than the earlier issues. A print from the original painting is shown above right.

Lids . . . . £25—£40
Plates . . . . . . £15—£30
Vases . . . . £40—£75

No. 357 The Irishman
First issued by F. & R. Pratt c.1850-60, from a painting by F. Goodall, details of which are given with No. 205, 'The Thirsty Soldier'. One size only and not seen on ware.

£30 — £50

No. 358 Little Red-riding Hood
A small lid produced by F. & R. Pratt c.1850, which, in common with many others, was produced over many years. Dessert ware was issued during the later period.

Lids £25 — £40   Plates £15 — £30

No. 359 The Red Bull Inn

A very popular subject by F. & R. Pratt, c.1860, produced over many years on a variety of items. Two varieties are known, either with or without the name 'Jonas Grubb' over the door; the later variety does not have the name. A medium sized lid, but is increased in size by the addition of a fancy border. Lids are known with extra seaweed design border and base. The original drawing by J. Austin shows the name over the door as 'Roger Grubb'; obviously this was altered by the engraver.

Medium or large, without name........ £25—£40
Medium or large, with name.......... £30—£50
Plates............................ £15—£30
Vases............................ *£100 plus*
Complete with seaweed border and base £75—£100

No. 360 Letter from the Diggings

F. & R. Pratt produced this lid in the early 1850s, at the time of the Australian gold-rush. Two sizes are known, with several varieties. The borders can be a line with a narrow fancy design, marbled, or a seaweed design. There are two very rare varieties; one with the wording 'Jules Hauel & Co., Perfumers, Philadelphia' round the border, and the other with the title 'Valentine's day', as seen in J. Austin's drawing. Obviously the engraver was instructed to make the necessary alteration for commercial reasons. A tall marbled pot and lid was produced for J. Gosnell, similar to No. 348, 'Peasant boys'. Later editions of this print are seen on ware and, in particular, on lids of powder bowls.

Lids................................	£25—£40	With wording 'Jules Hauel' etc..	P.B.N.
Marbled or mottled..................	£50—£75	Plates.......................	£15—£30
Complete on marbled or mottled pots...	£75—£100	Vases	£100 plus
With wording 'Valentine's day'........	P.B.N.	Powder bowls, etc.............	£30—£50

No. 361 The Wolf and the Lamb

Another lid by F. & R. Pratt, c.1860, and produced for many years. Medium size only, and not usually seen on ware.

£25 — £40

No. 362 Charity

An early lid from Cauldon, c.1850-60. The usual Cauldon creamy texture is very noticeable. Either medium or large, the medium size is printed completely to the edge of the lid, with the larger size having an extra white surround border. A further variety has coloured rims and bases to match.

Either medium or large................. £25—£50
Complete with coloured base............ £50—£75
*A small size has now been recorded with a
fancy decorative border.................* £60—£100

No. 363 The Listener

From F. & R. Pratt c.1850-60. The earliest editions do not have the fancy border seen on later issues. Screw-top lids are also known on the original issue. Varieties include marbled or seaweed decoration complete on bases. Two sizes are known, medium and large. Copied by J. Austin from Mayerheim's painting 'Trina' (left).

Medium or large . . . . £30—£50
Complete on seaweed base . . . . . . £60—£80
Complete on gold flecked pot . . . £75—£100

No. 364 The Strawberry Girl

A J. Austin copy from the painting by Sir Joshua Reynolds and produced by F. & R. Pratt, c.1850-60. Very great care must be exercised in acquiring this lid; the early editions are very scarce and later editions were produced 1880-90. Careful checking, with the details given in the Introduction will help the collector. A very popular subject, used on dessert ware.

Early issues........ *£125—£250*
Later issues........ *£50—£75*
Plates .... *£25—£50*

No. 365 The Waterfall

A lid produced in two sizes, medium and large, by F. & R. Pratt, c.1850-60, the larger size having a seaweed or marbled decorative border. A further variety has extra gold scroll decorative lines on lid and base. Also used on dessert ware.

Medium size	*£30—£50*
Large size, seaweed border	*£50—£75*
Large size, seaweed border, complete on pot	*£75—£100*
Gold scroll lines complete on pot	*£150—£300*
Plates	*£15—£30*

No. 366 Youth and Age

Produced originally c.1850-60 by the Mayer factory and later extensively copied by the various owners; such copies usually have an extra border. Reference to the Kirkham list (Appendix III) shows this lid to be one which was issued up to the 1960s. Not seen on any ware.

Early issues	*£125—£250*
Later issues	*£30—£50*
Reissue as Kirkhams	*£20—£30*

No. 367 How I Love to Laugh

A very early lid from an unknown factory. The jacket can be coloured red or green. There is a slight difference in technique with the usual underglaze colour printing for this lid. This particular lid is partly printed in outline, and completed by hand-colouring under the glaze before firing.

Either green or red jacket	*£150—£250*
Complete on marbled pot	*£200—£300*

Ware and Trinket Set Accessories

Nos. 369-378 were all produced by F. & R. Pratt for toilet requisites, c.1860-90.

No. 369 Fisherman's Abode
Extra small lid   £30—£50
Complete with pot   £40—£80

No. 370 The Round Tower
Extra small lid . . . .   £30—£50
Complete with decorative
pot . . . .   £40—£80

No. 371 Monastic Ruins
Extra small lid (white
surround) . . . .   £30—£40
Extra small lid (coloured
surround) . . . .   £30—£50
Complete with pot . . . . .   £40—£80

No. 372 The Shrine
Medium size lid (white
surround) . . . . £30—£40
Medium size lid (coloured
surround) . . . . £30—£50
Complete with pot . . . . . . £40—£80

No. 373 Ruined Temples
It is generally thought that the small hole seen in the lid is to hold a wax taper, which could be used to heat sealing wax when writing letters. The pot itself contained the tapers.

           Extra small lid   £30—£50
           Complete with pot   £40—£80

No. 375 The Toll Bridge
Tooth-brush holder £30 — £50
(agreed prices for other items)

No. 374 Medieval Mansion
Small lid	*£30—£50*
Complete with pot	*£40—£80*

No. 376
Ruined Abbey Chancel
Medium size lid (coloured
surround) . . . . £40—£60
Complete with pot . . . . £50—£100

No. 377 Watering Cattle
Medium size lid
(coloured surround) . . . . £40—£60
Complete with pot . . . . £50—£100

No. 377a Ruined Tower
Small size lid (white surround) . . . . £30—£40
Small size lid (coloured surround) . . . . £40—£60
Complete with pot . . . . £50—£80

No. 378 The Crooked Bridge

Like the items on the two preceding pages, these were produced by F. & R. Pratt c.1860-90 for toilet requisites.

    Trinket tray . . . . *£15—£25*
    Candlestick . . . . *£25—£40*
    Plaque 3¼ins. by 3¾ins. . . *£80—£125*
    (Agreed prices for other items)

No. 379 Bacchanalians at Play

A subject produced by the Mayer factory on a variety of wares c.1850-60. Two different prints were used, one showing three cherubs, the other showing five cherubs. Both these prints are seen on any item concerned. For instance, jugs have three cherubs on one face and five on the other.

Punch bowl	£75—£120
Extra decorative punch bowl	£125—£200
Plaques.....................	£80—£120
Jugs	£20—£40

(Differences according to condition and style)

One of the very fine bird plates by F. & R. Pratt with a rather unusual but attractive border.

An excellent example of a bread dish produced by F. & R. Pratt 1850-60.

A plate with a narrow, malachite border showing 'The Last In'. These are very scarce.

A very fine and highly decorated plaque by F. & R. Pratt. The example shown is marked with the date of production — 1853. A similar one is in the Victoria and Albert Museum.

No. 380 The Music Lesson

Both lids produced by T.J. & J. Mayer, and, to date, only one copy of each is known.

In 1934 a list of Mayer subjects was published in the *Exchange and Mart* of October 16th, and included in that list were the two lids mentioned here, and in 1936, No. 380, 'The Music Lesson' (originally called 'The Arcadians'), was discovered, which led to hopes that the companion lid would soon be found. However, in the event, this particular lid did not appear for nearly another forty years, and it was not until 1974 that the two lids were brought together again.

No. 380 may be illustrating Shakespeare's lines on Orpheus and Eurydice.

Either lid P.B.N.

No. 380a Maidens Decorating Bust of Homer

Nos. 381-424 were produced by F. & R. Pratt at Fenton, c.1860-90. Earlier and later editions are mentioned as needed. All items are in a variety of colours, such as maroon, red, green, blue, yellow, etc., blue and yellow being rarer than the other colours.

No. 381 The Cavalier and The Serving Woman

Oblong lid	*£30—£50*	*Jugs*	*£15—£30*
Lid and base ..	*£40—£60*	*Tobacco jars* ..	*£50—£80*
Cups	*£15—£30*	*Tankards*	*£50—£80*

No. 382 The Cattle Drover

Oblong lid	*£30—£50*	*Mugs*	*£20—£40*
Lid and base . . .	*£40—£60*	*Tea-pots*	*£30—£50*

No. 383 Continental Scene

Oblong lid	*£30—£50*	*Trinket tray*	*£15—£25*	*Cup*	*£15—£30*
Lid and base	*£40—£60*	*Tea-pot*	*£30—£50*	*Coffee can*	*£15—£30*

No. 384 The Deer-stalker

No. 385 The Wild Deer

The prints on these two oblong pot-lids are taken from drawings by Landseer and are the same as those on jars 92 and 92A. The Landseer originals are shown top right and left.

Either lid   *£50—£75*
Lid and base   *£60—£100*

No. 386 The Donkey's Foal
The original painting by Park entitled 'Returning from the Moors' is shown above.

Oblong lid   *£30—£40*
Lid and base   *£40—£60*

No. 387 Driving Cattle

Oblong lid ...... *£30—£50* *Cup* .... *£15—£30*
Lid and base .... *£40—£60* *Mug* .... *£20—£40*
Tobacco jar £50 — £80

No. 388 Cows in Stream near Ruins

Oblong lid . . . . . . £30—£50	*Sugar basin* . . . £25—£40
Lid and base . . . . £40—£60	*Loving cup* . . . £25—£40
Tobacco jar . . . . . £50—£80	*Bowl* . . . . £20—£30

No. 389 The Ferry Boat

Oblong lid	*£40—£60*	*Tea-pot*	*£30—£50*
Lid and base	*£50—£75*	*Sugar basin*	*£20—£30*
Cream jug	*£15—£25*		

No. 390 Halt near Ruins

Oblong lid	*£30—£50*	*Sugar basin*	*£20—£30*
Lid and base	*£40—£60*	*Mug*	*£20—£30*
Cream jug	*£15—£25*		

No. 391 Milking the Cow
See also No. 86.

Oblong lid	£30—£40
Lid and base.............	£40—£60
Coloured lid and base	£50—£75

No. 392 The Muleteer

Oblong lid	£30—£50	Jug	£15—£25
Lid and base	40—£60	Tankard	£50—£80
Mug	£20—£30	Cup	£15—£30

No. 393 A Sea-shore Study

See also No. 96A. Print from Stothard's painting is shown above.

Oblong lid	*£30—£40*
Lid and base	*£40—£60*

No. 394 The Stone Bridge

Oblong lid	*£30—£50*	*Sugar basin*	*£20—£30*
Lid and base	*£40—£60*	*Cup*	*£15—£30*
Cream jug	*£15—£25*		

No. 395 The Stone Jetty
Many later issues of this lid and base are known; these are recognisable by the light-weight ware and pale printing. See also No. 89.

Oblong lid	£30—£40
Lid and base	£40—£60
Bowl	£20—£30
Mug	£20—£30
Cup	£15—£30
Tray	£20—£30
Late issues lid and base	£15—£30
Nos. 395 and 396 shown on a pair of spill vases	£50—£75

No. 396
The Traveller's Departure

Very late issues are known, see
No. 395. See also No. 82.

Oblong lid	£30—£40
Lid and base	£40—£60
Cup	£15—£30
Tobacco jar	£50—£80
Mug	£20—£30
Vase	£30—£50
Bowl	£20—£30
Late issues lid and base	£15—£30
Nos. 395 and 396 shown on a pair of spill vases	£50—£75

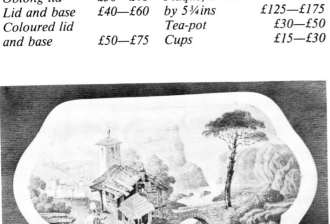

No. 397 Tyrolese Village Scene

Oblong lid	£30—£40	Plaque, 6¾ins.	
Lid and base	£40—£60	by 5¾ins	£125—£175
Coloured lid		Tea-pot	£30—£50
and base	£50—£75	Cups	£15—£30

No. 398 Village Scene on the Continent

Oblong lid	£30—£40	Tea-pots	£30—£50
Lid and base	£40—£60	Cups	£15—£30
Plaque, 6¾ins.		Two-handled	
by 5¾ins.	£125—£175	loving cup	£40—£75

No. 399 The Windmill

Oblong lid	£30—£40	Cups	£15—£30
Lid and base	£40—£60	Mugs	£20—£30

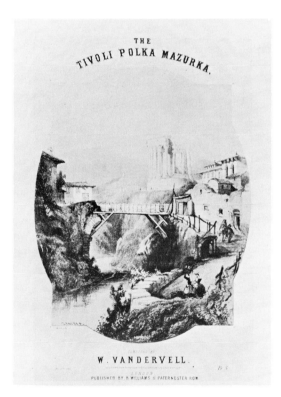

No. 400 The Wooden Bridge

The print above is a Victorian music sheet cover, printed in reverse to the engraving for the copper plates used for this subject.

Oblong lid	£30—£40	Jugs	£15—£25
Lid and base	£40—£60	Tobacco jars	£50—£80
Bowls	£20—£30	Sugar basins	£20—£30
Two-handled		Mugs	£20—£30
loving cups	£40—£75	Vases	£30—£50

No. 400
The Wooden Bridge
See caption
on page 245

**No. 401 Uncle Tom
and Eva**

No. 402 Uncle Tom

See also No. 91.

Either lid	*£80—£120*
Lid and	
base	*£125—£175*
Vases	*£200 plus*
Long necked	
bottles	*£100—£150*

No. 403   Horse Drawing Boat to Land

Oblong lid	£30—£50	*Bowls*	£20—£30
Lid and base	£50—£75	*Sugar basins*	£20—£30
Mugs	£20—£30	*Vases*	£30—£50

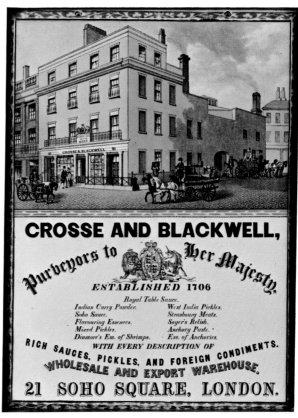

Left and above: Two advertising plaques (referred to as tiles in the advertisements of c.1850-60). Manufactured by T.J. & J. Mayer, these items are now extremely rare.

Above and right: Three unusual triangular shaped bottles and a rare advertising plaque by F. & R. Pratt.

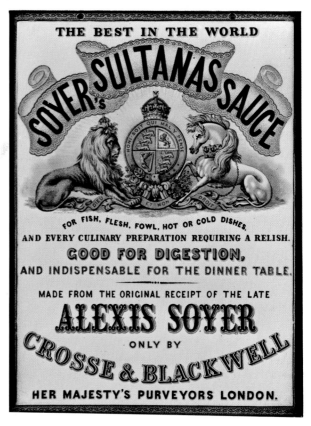

No. 404 Passing the Pipe

Any lid	£75—£100
Lid and base	£100—£175
Bowls	£30—£40
Mugs	£40—£60
Tobacco jars	£80—£120
Two-handled loving cups	£50—£80
Spill vases (404, 405, 406)	£30—£40
Set of three spill vases	£100—£150
Cups	£20—£40

No. 405 The Smokers

Spill vases with this print usually do not show the shuttered window seen on the right of other items bearing this print.

Any lid	*£75—£100*
Lid and base.............................	*£100—£175*
Bowls	*£30—£40*
Mugs.....................................	*£40—£60*
Tobacco jars	*£80—£120*
Two-handled loving cups	*£50—£80*
Spill vases...............................	*£30—£40*
Set of three spill vases (404, 405, 406)	*£100—£150*
Cups	*£20—£40*

No. 406 Jolly Topers

Any lid	*£75—£100*
Lid and base	*£100—£175*
Bowls	*£30—£40*
Mugs	*£40—£60*
Tobacco jars	*£80—£120*
Two-handled loving cups	*£50—£80*
Spill vases	*£30—£40*
Set of three spill vases (404, 405, 406)	*£100—£150*
Cups	*£20—£40*

No. 407 View near St. Michael's Mount

Oblong lid	*£30—£40*
Lid and base	*£40—£60*
Mugs	*£20—£30*
Tea-pots	*£30—£50*

No. 408 A Rhine Scene
Tobacco jars £100 plus

No. 409 Bridge across the Gap
Butter dish and cover . . . . . £30—£40
Candlestick . . . . £25—£40
Ring stand . . . . £20—£30
Trinket pot complete . . . . . . £25—£40

No. 410
Tyrolese Hill Scene
Butter dish and cover   £30—£40
Trinket pot complete   £25—£40

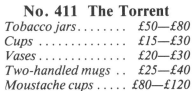

No. 411   The Torrent
Tobacco jars........   £50—£80
Cups ....   £15—£30
Vases ....   £20—£30
Two-handled mugs ..   £25—£40
Moustache cups .....   £80—£120

No. 412 The Last In

A print of Mulready's painting is shown for comparison.

Large lid and base, 7½ins. diameter	*P.B.N.*
Narrow malachite border plate	*£100—£150*
Wide malachite border plate	*£80—£100*
Wide malachite border comport	*£80—£120*
(Tall) wide malachite border comport	*£100—£150*
Wide acorn border plate	*£60—£80*
Wide acorn border plate with gold scroll	*£60—£100*
Wide acorn border comport	*£75—£100*
Wide acorn border comport with gold scroll	*£75—£120*
White surround pharmacy jar top, 11¼ins. diameter	*£50—£75*
White surround bread dishes	*£60—£80*

No. 413 The Truant

A print of Webster's painting is shown for comparison.

Large malachite lid and base, 7½ins.	
diameter	P.B.N.
Malachite border plate	£80—£100
Malachite border comport	£80—£120
Acorn border plate	£60—£80
Acorn border plate with gold scroll	£60—£100
Acorn border comport	£75—£100
Acorn border comport with gold scroll	£75—£120
Comports and plates with various borders	
and colours	£30—£60
Large malachite jugs	P.B.N.
Plaques	£30—£50
Globular pharmacy jars	£100—£150

No. 414 The Hop Queen

A print of Withrington's painting is shown for comparison.

Large malachite lid and base, 7½ ins. diameter	*P.B.N.*
Malachite border plate	*£80—£100*
Malachite border comport	*£80—£120*
Acorn border plate	*£60—£80*
Acorn border comport	*£75—£100*
Acorn border plates with gold scroll	*£60—£100*
Acorn border comports with gold scroll ...	*£75—£120*
Comports and plates with various colours and borders	*£30—£50*
Pharmacy jars	*£100—£150*

No. 415 The Bully

A print of the painting by Mulready is shown for
reference. The actual title of the painting, 'The Wolf
and the Lamb', is not used for this subject, but is used
for the lid, No. 361.

Malachite border plate	*£80—£100*
Acorn border plate	*£60—£80*
Acorn border plate with gold scroll	*£60—£100*
Malachite jug	*P.B.N.*
Plaques	*£30—£50*
Plates with various borders	*£30—£50*

No. 416 Landscape and River Scene
*Plates and comports with various
borders and colours* . . . . *£20—£40*

No. 417 The Blind Fiddler

The details of the vase shown above are the same as those for No. 313, 'Cottage Children', on page 285.

Malachite border comport	£80—£120
Acorn border comport	£75—£100
Acorn border comport with gold scroll	£75—£120
Comport with maroon ground and decorative handles	£50—£75
Oval plaque	£30—£50
Vase	P.B.N.

No. 418 Highland Music
A print of Landseer's painting is shown for comparison.

Malachite border comport . . . . . . *£80—£120*
Acorn border comport . . . . *£75—£100*
Acorn border comport with gold
scroll . . . . *£75—£120*
Oval plaque . . . . *£30—£50*

No. 419 The Travelling Knife-grinder
A print of Tenier's painting, which was used on the
cover of the Penny Magazine, is shown for comparison.
Plates with various coloured borders £20 — £40

No. 420 Roman Ruins
Late issue large size lid, 4¾ins.
diameter .... £100 plus
Plates with various colours and borders .... £20—£40

No. 421 The Ruined Temple
Plates with various colours and borders £20 — £40

No. 422 The Rustic Laundrywoman

Large size lid, 4¾ins. diameter .... £100 plus
Plates and dishes with various borders and
colours.............................. £20—£40

No. 423 The Mountain Stream

Large ewers . . . . £50—£75
Comports, dishes and plates with various
colours and borders . . . . £20—£40
Bread dish . . . . £40—£75

No. 424 Christ in the Cornfield

One of the large plaques, heightened in gold, is displayed in the Victoria and Albert Museum.

Bread dishes with various coloured surrounds .... £80—£120

Large plaques, 13ins. diameter, heightened in gold .... £200-£300

Similar plaques with malachite border .... 200—£300

Bread dishes with gold scroll embellishments .... £250—£350

A child's miniature dinner and tea set showing scenes of Windsor Castle with the two royal children — H.R.H. the Prince of Wales and H.R.H. the Princess Royal.

No. 425 The Poultry Yard, Trentham

These three very fine prints, Nos. 425, 426 and 427 (shown on page 270), were produced by the Mayer factory on plates c.1880-90. Three different issues of Nos. 425 and 426 are known: (a) in porcelain with cerise colourings (printed overglaze); (b) in pottery with elaborate gold finishings; and (c) in pottery with scroll border. The Trentham plates may have been manufactured for the Duke and Duchess of Sutherland, who were in residence at Trentham Hall during that period.

(a)   £75—£100
(b)   £150—£200
(c)   £50—£75
Flask with vine leaf border P.B.N.

No. 426 Trentham Hall

No. 426 Trentham Hall

No. 427 Monastery in Alton Towers

See caption on page 269

No. 428 A Rural Scene

A Pratt subject on various items of ware. A close look at the cottage, figures and trees in the background shows that they are identical to those in No. 419, 'The Travelling Knife-grinder'.

Dessert plates	*£20—£40*
Saucers	*£15—£25*
Tea pot stands	*£30—£40*
Late issue large size lids, 4¾ins. diameter	*£100+*

No. 429 Fruit, Glass and Wine Decanter

An underglaze colour-printed plate by Morgan, Wood and Co., c.1860-70. Reference to Nos. 295 and 295B shows those two items to be produced at the same factory, when in the ownership of Wood and Baggaley. The factory marks are shown for reference, both on Nos. 295, 295B and this plate, No. 429.

£25 — £40

No. 430 Tremadoc

One of a series of four plates produced by F.& R. Pratt c.1860, the others being Haddon Hall, Hafod and Chatsworth (Nos. 435-437). Many late issues are seen of all these plates, even up to, and including the early years of this century, when Cauldon reissued the series, after acquiring the copper plates from F. & R. Pratt, as part of the assets. The early issues have a very fine border of classical design, with an outer coloured line, usually either blue or red. The later issues do not have this classical design border; it is usually a coloured ground with the 123 border (see Glossary), and the ware is a much finer body.

Tremadoc is a small market town close to Portmadoc, both towns taking their name from a Mr. Maddocks, M.P., who, in the early 19th century, played a leading part in establishing both towns on land reclaimed from the sea.

Early issue	*£50—£75*
Later issue	*£20—£40*

No. 431 The Spanish Dancers
See No. 250, 'Fair Sportswoman', for all details.
Plates or comports £20 — £40

No. 432 The Two Anglers
Produced on a variety of wares by F. & R. Pratt, c.1860-80. A number of different borders and colourings are known to have been used as decoration for this subject, examples of which are shown.

Plates . . . . £20—£40
Ewers . . . . £50—£75
Bread dishes . . . £40—£75

No. 433 Grecian Landscape
A small oblong subject seen only on wares, usually of a very late period. Cups and plates have been seen, after the takeover of F. & R. Pratt c.1920.

Any kind of ware £20 — £30

No. 434 Dressing My Lady's Hair
Originally produced by T.J. & J. Mayer, c.1860, for use on an advertising plaque for 'Rowland's Macassar Oil', a plaque which is exceptional for its brilliant colouring. Later issued on a large sized lid, c.1880, with colouring not of the quality seen on the plaque. The plaque forms a trio with Nos. 452 and 453.

Lid £100 plus   Plaque P.B.N.

No. 435 Haddon Hall

No. 436 Hafod

No. 437 Chatsworth

Nos. 435, 436 and 437
See No. 430, 'Tremadoc', for full details of these plates.
Early issues £50—£75
Late issues £20—£40

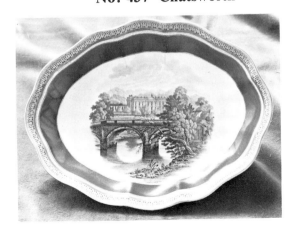

No. 438 Unwelcome Attentions
An early subject from an unknown factory, c.1850-60.
A very scarce item, usually seen on plaques.
P.B.N.

No. 439A Bouquet

No. 439B Bouquet

No. 439 Bouquet

A dessert service which has the three subjects shown, repeated to form the complete service. A very attractive design, usually with a harebell border, heightened in gold. Other borders are known — a leaf design in various colours and a scroll design, also touched with various colours.

Plates and comports £25 — £40

No. 439B Bouquet

No. 439C Bouquet

No. 440 Chinese River Scene, with Junks

An extremely fine pair of small vases, 5½ins. high, from F. & R. Pratt.

Single vases	*P.B.N.*
Pair vases	*P.B.N.*

No. 441 Roman Ruins and Pedestrians

A subject by F. & R. Pratt, used on toilet ware, trinket trays in particular, known in a variety of ground laid colours.

Trinket trays	*£15—£30*
Candlesticks	*£15—£30*

No. 442
Crosse and Blackwell's Advertising Plaque
A very colourful advertising plaque produced by T.J. & J. Mayer, c.1850. Two varieties of this plaque are known; there are slight differences, such as the number of people shown, the horse and cart facing in different directions, and the smoke from the chimney blows in different directions. Varieties are seen with the lower half of the plaque in either blue, pink or white, and some show a different number of products advertised for sale.

P.B.N.

No. 443 The Milkmaid
See No. 350, 'Halt by the Wayside', for details.

Plates	£15—£30
Tea-pot stands	£15—£30
Bowls	£15—£30
Lids	£50—£80

No. 444 Philadelphia Public Building 1876

No. 444A Interior View, Independence Hall, Philadelphia

A series of four plates produced by F. & R. Pratt, possibly at the time of the Philadelphia Exhibition of 1876, which was held in celebration of the Declaration of Independence in 1776.

The usual 123 border is replaced by a star and stripe motif, except for No. 444A. In addition to the mark of F. & R. Pratt & Co. on the underside, the name of R.T. Allen, the agent in Philadelphia, will often be seen.

Any plate £40 — £60

No. 444B State House in Philadelphia 1776

No. 444C Philadelphia Exhibition 1876

No. 445 The Stall-woman

See No. 350, 'Halt by the Wayside', for details.

Plates	£15—£30	Cups	£15—£30
Tea-pot stands	*£15—£30*	*Saucers*	*£15—£30*

No. 446 Soyer's Advertising Plaque

A similar plaque to No. 442 and equally as colourful, the colours used being purple, red, brown, black and gold. Produced by F. & R. Pratt, for Messrs. Crosse & Blackwell, c.1850, it is signed 'Designed & engraved by J. Austin'. The dimensions are approximately 12ins. by 10ins., and only one copy of this plaque is known to be in existence.

P.B.N.

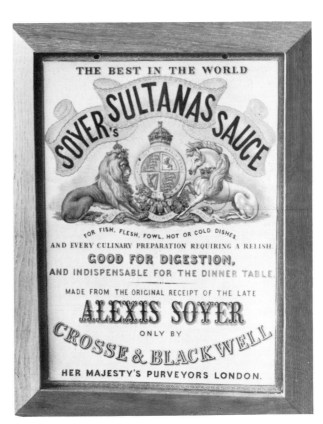

No. 447 Royal Children — Windsor Castle

A subject in two designs, used as the central motif on children's dinner and tea services, showing the two Royal children being taken for a ride round the grounds of Windsor Castle in a goat-cart. Thought to have been produced by T.J. & J. Mayer, c.1855.

Cups, saucers or plates	*£10—£15*
Tea-pots	*£15—£30*
Complete tea service	*£150—£250*
Dishes, tureens, gravy boats	*£10—£15*
Complete 60 piece dinner service	*£400—£500*

No. 448a **No. 448a**

No. 448 Ecclesiastical Subjects
See caption on page 281

No. 448a

No. 448b

No. 448 Ecclesiastical Subjects
Subjects which were produced by F. & R. Pratt, to be
used on toilet ware of the period.

(a)	Soap dish	£25—£40
(a)	Toothbrush holder ..	£25—£40
(b)	Sponge dish	£30—£50
(c)	Chamber pot	£30—£50
(d)	Tile	£20—£30
(e)	Jug...............	£15—£30

No. 448c

No. 448d

No. 448e

No. 449 Birds

Similar marks and designs as mentioned in the section on No. 52, 'Shells'. Most likely produced c.1860 by Cockson and Harding, whose colour printing is usually inferior to either Pratt or Mayer. The mark on the base is shown.

£10 — £25

No. 450 Royal Coat of Arms
(J. Gosnell & Co.)

An unusual application of a multicoloured plaque, probably produced by Mayer, for John Gosnell and Co., who at the time also manufactured hair brushes under their patent name Trichosaron.

A small plaque on the reverse side of the handle gives the address of John Gosnell and Co. as 12, Three King Court, Lombard Street, London, which premises were gutted by fire in 1865. The date of the plaque can, therefore, safely be dated as 1865 or earlier.

Another variety has been seen with a different Coat of Arms, probably produced by F. & R. Pratt.

£60 — £80

No. 451 Grapes, Hazelnuts and Medlar

A very attractive plate by F. & R. Pratt, which shows a colourful assortment of leaves and fruit, the whole being surrounded with attractive borders in pink and gold.

The dictionary definition of a 'Medlar' is a rosaceous tree, the fruit of which is eaten when beginning to decay.

The only copy known.

P.B.N.

No. 452 Rowland's Odonto

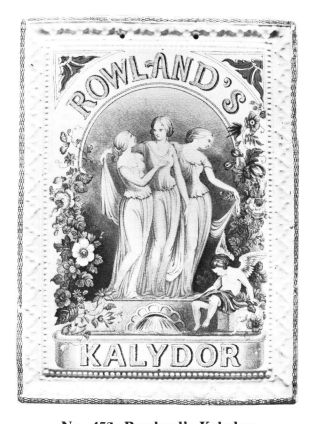

No. 453 Rowland's Kalydor

Two colourful advertising plaques from T.J. & J. Mayer, issued c.1860. These two plaques complete a trio with the equally colourful plaque No. 434 'Dressing my Lady's Hair', advertising 'Rowland's Macasser Oil'.

Price for either plaque: P.B.N.

Additional Items

No. 454 Jewsbury & Brown Plate

A floral plate, advertising 'Jewsbury & Brown's Oriental Toothpaste'. Printed in monochrome with the colours red, yellow, green and blue being hand applied. Possibly produced by Brown, Westhead, Moore and Co., in the latter part of the 19th century.

£40 — £60

No. 455 Huntley and Palmer's Plaque

An advertising plaque which has not previously been recorded. Produced by T.J. & J. Mayer c.1850, possibly for the 1851 Exhibition, where Huntley & Palmer's had a stand which not only displayed their products, but also showed the method of production.

Unfortunately, this surviving example of fine multicolour printing on an advertising plaque has been damaged by the removal of the lower half, which, no doubt, had details of the products on sale at that date.

P.B.N.

No. 456 Eugenie

An attractive lid, not, strictly speaking, multicoloured. A monochrome lid with a yellow colour wash giving a very attractive appearance. Manufacturers unknown, possibly manufactured c.1850-60.

£30 — £50

No. 457 Crosse & Blackwell Plaque

Black print, made of porcelain, no potter's mark, 10¼ins. x 8ins. overall.

P.B.N.

No. 458 The Two Bears

A pot-lid in two colours besides black, namely pale blue and pink, with stippling used on all black and blue areas. There are no stilt marks and the surface is slightly domed. 2¾ins. diameter.

P.B.N.

No. 459 A Good Catch

A barrel shaped jar, 3¼ins. high, bearing four colours, brown, blue, red and yellow, the printing in brown (all under the glaze). There are no other marks and the print is on one side only.

P.B.N.

No. 313 Cottage Children

A print of the 'Cottage Children' is seen on a very unusual vase bearing the mark of Prince Albert, which means that it was produced before 1861 by F. & R. Pratt & Co. There is a similar vase with a print of No. 417, the 'Blind Fiddler'. The body is transfer printed in simulated malachite but with a predominantly darker green composition. See other items on page 188.

P.B.N.

Three plates showing old English scenes and printed by the multicolour process by Wm. Smith, Stockton-on-Tees c.1850. Occasionally to be seen with the name Wedgwood impressed on the underside.

A view in the Highlands, seen on a tea-pot stand and possibly produced by G.L. Ashworth, c.1860-70.

Glossary

AUSTIN, JESSE

Jesse Austin was born in Longton, Stoke-on-Trent, Staffordshire on February 5th, 1806, his father owning a tailoring business in that town. On leaving Longton Grammar School, Austin was apprenticed to Davenports China Works to learn the art of engraving. After completing his apprenticeship, he received several set-backs in his career until he eventually joined F. & R. Pratt, High Street, Fenton, Stoke-on-Trent, with whom he remained, except for a short period of twelve months or so, for the rest of his working life. He died, aged 73, at Fenton on March 30th, 1879 and was buried in St. Paul's Churchyard, Longton.

Several different varieties of Jesse Austin's signature were used, sometimes in conjunction with the name of the painter: 'J.A.', 'J.A. Sc.', 'J. AUSTIN, Sc.', 'J. AUSTIN, INV'.

BORDERS

A vignette is a print not enclosed within a definite border.

The 123 border. A border seen only on items from the Pratt factory, the motif of which is a Greek key pattern; this print was No. 123 in the factory pattern book. Wherever the numerals occur printed on an item, that particular item will invariably carry the border, although occasionally items do not carry the number. If the border is used on late items, it is always very pale in colour. See No. 407, View near St. Michael's Mount', on the teapot. With additional gilt scroll border, see No. 428, 'A rural scene', on the plate.

The harebell border. See No. 365 'The Waterfall', on the plate.

The bouquet series (No. 439) has a border very similar to the harebell, on the plates and comport. Variations of the bouquet have either a small leaf pattern or a decorative scroll design, also seen on No. 439.

'Cherub' borders. A classical design of cherubs at play. See No. 432, 'The Two Anglers', on one of the plates.

Malachite border, see No. 414, 'The Hop Queen', on pot-lid with base and one variety of plate.

Acorn border, see No. 412, 'The Last In' on the comport and one of the plates. (This print is sometimes greatly enhanced by the backing of gilt scrollwork.)

Classical border. A border showing reclining figures, see No. 430, 'Tremadoc', on the plate.

Griffin border, see No. 416, 'Landscape and River Scene', on one of the plates.

Cherub and Classical border, see No. 431, 'Spanish Dancers'.

Pearl dot border, see No. 278, 'The Robin', on the plate.

Stars and Stripes border, see No. 444B, 'State House in Philadelphia 1776'.

Crackle border, see No. 217, 'Conway Castle', on the comport and plate.

Gilt scroll border, see No. 441, 'Roman Ruins and Pedestrians', on the trinket tray.

Floral border, see No. 131/10, on the plate.

DISTRIBUTORS' MARKS

Names or marks often seen on the underside of ware, refer either to the manufacturer of the product packed in the container, or to the retailer/wholesaler who was responsible for distributing these items. Three such items are shown in plates i, ii and iii. See also Manufacturers' Marks.

F. & R. PRATT & Cº
FENTON
STAFFORDSHIRE

Plate i

Plate ii

Plate iii

Plate iv

DRAWINGS
There are a number of drawings by Jesse Austin still in existence of which no lids have yet been seen. This drawing by him (plate iv) is one of these, and it is possible that some day a lid may be found showing this drawing.

MANUFACTURERS' MARKS
Lids are normally not marked, but very late lids are sometimes seen with the wording 'PRATT—FENTON' printed in brown on the underside. An unusual mark, occasionally seen, from F. & R. Pratt, and only used on ware, is shown on plate v. Another mark often used was the one shown on plate vi; this particular mark was withdrawn after the death of Prince Albert in 1861. The number, 123, seen on the underside of ware, always refers to the border on items from F. & R. Pratt. A printed number in black, on the underside, denotes a lid from the Mayer factory. Reissues of this century often have the inscriptions shown in plates vii and viii. These are the lids of which collectors must be wary, especially if the back is filled in or covered over with either paint or material such as plaster. See also Distributors' Marks.

Plate v

Plate vi

Plate vii

Plate viii

MONOCHROME PRINTING
Collectors always find it difficult to know where to draw the dividing line between monochrome, duo-tone or multicolour printed lids, and it is common knowledge that there are literally thousands of monochrome advertising lids in existence. However, it is not intended to trespass on the preserves of monochrome printed lids, but the following few notes and photographs may help in deciding in which category a lid should be placed, omitting all purely advertising lids and showing only pictorial or coloured subjects. The items shown were all produced contemporary with the multicolour subjects and are printed in one colour only, mainly black. Other colours are known, such as 'Old Jack' and 'A Rebel', which were printed in brown and also in green.

'A Hero' or 'Jack at Uncle Majors'

'A Rebel' or 'Jack at Old Birch's'

Eridge Castle near Tunbridge Wells

Chichester Cathedral

Petworth House, Sussex

Castle Highclere, near Newbury, Berks

Christ Church, Hants

The High Street and New Church of St. Nicholas, Guildford

Haddon Hall

Building for the Great Exhibition 1851

Chain Pier, Brighton

Canterbury Cathedral

Berwick border bridge

Lymington Church (two varieties)

Three Choristers

Faith, Hope and Charity

Jars and other items were also produced using the same process, examples of which are shown:—

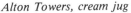

The Great Exhibition of 1851, mug (possibly produced by G.F. Bowers of Tunstall Staffs., who produced and showed this type of mug at the 1851 Exhibition).

Alton Towers, cream jug *Atherstone Church, spill vase*

Ann Hathaway's Cottage, meat past jar

Holy Trinity Church, meat paste jar

Shakespeare's House, meat paste jar

A slightly different process produced lids in more than one colour. This was achieved by printing the outline (as mentioned previously) in black, or some suitable colour, and then covering the print with either a solid ground print or a colour-wash by hand. Another method was to print the outline and then fill in the required colours by hand, overglaze, and this method is still being used. Examples of both these methods are shown:—

Dr. Dosteel's Cherry Tooth Paste, pink ground

Swift's Hair Regenerator, pink and bronze ground

Gosnell's Cherry Tooth Paste, grey and bronze ground

290

Thompson, Walters, Hole & Co., Cherry Tooth Paste, yellow ground, red cherries, green leaves, partially hand-painted.

Bedford's Honeysuckle Tooth Paste, fawn ground

Stone's Cherry Tooth Paste, pink ground

Anchovy paste, cream ground

Cherry Blossom toilet powder, pink ground

Right: Crystal Palace, gilt scroll-work, overglaze print. This particular lid has always been classified as hand-painted. This statement is not correct; it is a print, but is printed overglaze and not underglaze, which gives the effect of painting, as with Nos. 425 and 426 (classification (a)), which are on porcelain, as is this Crystal Palace lid and base.

A later and more economical method was by means of overglaze colour lithographic transfer-printing. This can be seen in the following examples:—

Lord Roberts (2 varieties)

R.S.S. Baden-Powell (2 varieties)

The Sirdar (Lord Kitchener)

General Buller

Lord Salisbury

Tom Ellis M.P.

Mr. Gladstone

Mrs. Gladstone

Queen Victoria (1897 Jubilee)

Desert scene (2 varieties)

Plate ix

PAPER LABELS

An early method of showing details on lids was by using paper labels, similar to the one shown (plate ix).

PRATT, FELIX EDWARDS

Felix Edwards Pratt was born in 1813 in Fenton, Stoke-on-Trent, where his family were established potters. His father, also named Felix Pratt, already had a flourishing pottery manufacturing business and had built up a reputation for producing wares decorated in rather stronger colours than had previously been used. This situation causes some minor confusion, even today, when certain early hand-painted wares are described as 'Pratt' and we have the later colour transfer decorated wares also known as 'Pratt wares', these being produced by F. & R. Pratt. Felix Edwards Pratt worked very closely with Jesse Austin all his working life, and died aged 81 years, being buried in Hartshill, Stoke-on-Trent.

REGISTRATION

'Entered at Stationers Hall'. Four lids bear this inscription, No. 186 'The Tower of London', No. 189 'Westminster Abbey', No. 192 'St. Paul's Cathedral', and No. 195 'New Houses of Parliament'. This was an act passed in 1735, to protect engravers from copyists. However, this act was amended in 1766 to allow engravers to copy any picture, drawing or sculpture, but this amendment was again amended in 1777 to permit any aggrieved person to sue for damages.

'The Design Act'. An act passed in 1842, which enabled a manufacturer to register and protect his own individual design or pattern, is seen on several lids, with the name of the person registering such design. Only the lids which actually show the design in the print or on the reverse, are described:

No.	Title	Registered by	Date
50	Injury	Bates, Elliott & Co.	June 11th 1873
51	Revenge	Bates, Elliott & Co.	June 11th 1873
168	Allied Generals	F. & R. Pratt & Co.	December 29th 1854
236	Parish Beadle	Thos. Jackson	July 1st 1852
238	Xmas Eve	Thos. Jackson	November 17th 1851
240	The Village Wedding	F. & R. Pratt & Co.	January 15th 1857
241	Our Home	Thos. Jackson	March 29th 1852
242	Our Pets	Thos. Jackson	March 29th 1852
246	Blind Man's Buff	F. & R. Pratt & Co.	November 7th 1856
253	Snap-dragon	F. & R. Pratt & Co.	August 12th 1856
297	The Swallow	Bates, Elliott & Co.	December 17th 1870
339	The Vine Girl	Bates, Elliott & Co.	January 1st 1874
342	Summer	Bates Elliott & Co.	January 1st 1874
342A	Autumn	Bates Elliott & Co.	January 1st 1874

The design is the diamond shaped figure, which was used between the years 1842-83 inclusive, and can be referred to in many antique reference books.

Thos. Jackson, was a manufacturing chemist of Manchester, who used the designs on pots containing his own manufactured products.

Designs registered by Bates, Elliott & Co., are all printed on the underside, and not shown incorporated in the print, as are the ones registered by F. & R. Pratt.

Any of the lids or ware mentioned, which do not show the design, are presumed to have been produced after 1883, the date on which the diamond-shaped design ceased to be used.

REISSUES

In addition to the warnings already given in the Introduction of this book concerning late or reissue lids, there are still pitfalls for the unwary, which can be avoided by reference to the following remarks and to the list as detailed.

Cauldon Potteries reissued lids and ware after the acquisition of F. & R. Pratt in 1920, up to and including the 1930s, but there are still later issues which have not at present ever been recorded, and it is hoped that the following information may help anyone who has experienced the problem of deciding the authenticity of these items.

In 1949 H.G. Clarke published his *Centenary Pot-lid Book,* and as a result was asked to give a television interview. During that interview he made a statement that the production of 'underglaze multicolour prints' was a lost art and could not be produced today, i.e. 1949. The Managing Director of Cauldon at that time was Stanley Harrison, who happened to hear about this interview and decided to see if this method of colour-transfer printing was completely lost. The Cauldon combine, including Coalport, was by this time operating from the factory of Geo. Jones Crescent Pottery at Stoke-on-Trent, and it was from this factory that these later reissues were made in the early 1950s. At first they were produced on the familiar 'Cauldon Ivory Body Earthenware', using differently embossed shapes for dessert ware and plates. Later it was decided to produce these items on china only, and this was continued until production ceased, approximately 1958, when the business of Coalport and Cauldon China was sold to Mr. E.M. Brain of Foley China, Fenton. The copper plates in the possession of Stanley Harrison were included in the sale and remained so, until Wedgwood's bought all the assets of Mr. Brain in 1967. This information now completes the history and story of the copper plates engraved by J. Austin at the factory of F. & R. Pratt, up to their present resting place in Coalport's factory at Stoke-on-Trent.

In presenting this list of the items reissued, the titles are as shown in Coalport's catalogue.

10ins. Plates and 8ins. Plates
Houses and scenes on assorted embossed shape:
Haddon Hall
LangollenTremadoc
Sandringham
Chatsworth
Strathfieldsaye
Hafod
The Two Anglers

Other Plates and embossed shapes (various):
Birds
Cuckoo
Thrush
Wren
Red Warbler
Blue and Long-tailed Tit
Robin
Owl
Bullfinch and Canary
Exotic Bird and Snakes
Eagle and Prey
Sea Eagle
Eagle

Victorian Series:
Victoria and Albert
Late Duke of Wellington
Allied Generals
England's Pride
The Late Prince Consort
Sir Robert Peel
Crystal Palace
Sebastopol
Embarking for the East
Albert Memorial
Wimbledon July 2nd 1860
H.R.H. The Prince of Wales
visiting the tomb of
Washington at Mt. Vernon

London Scenes:
Thames Embankment
Holborn Viaduct
Charing Cross
Blackfriars Bridge
Albert Memorial
St. Paul's and River Pageant
The New St. Thomas's Hospital
Trafalgar Square

Shakespeare Scenes:
Shakespeare's House
Room in which Shakespeare was born 1564
Ann Hathaway's Cottage
Church of the Holy Trinity
Seven Ages of Man
Hamlet and his Father's Ghost (see plate x).

Gadroon Sweets:
Birds as previously listed and The Faithful Shepherd and The Old Water-mill

Tankards:
The Reception of H.R.H. The Prince of Wales at London Bridge March 7th 1863
The Meet of the Fox Hounds
Round Candy Boxes:
London Scenes as previously listed and a variety of other scenes

Other Prints used on 10ins. Plates:
Heron
Hop Queen
The Bully
The Truant
Oval Dessert Dish Regency
Highland Music
Large Round Dish, Regency
The Last In
Oblong Tray, Regency
Various Prints

SIGNATURES see Austin, Jesse.

Plate x

APPENDIX I

COPPER PLATES AT COALPORT

Set out below is a comprehensive list of copper plates at Coalport. Collectors are indebted to H.G. Clarke who first numbered the lids as on the copper plates at the Cauldon factory in the early 1920s, these being the combined plates of F. & R. Pratt and Cauldon. In 1955, H.G. Clarke revised these numbers, as prints from other factories were discovered. Further revision was made on the publication of *The Price Guide to Pot-Lids* in 1970; this was found necessary as yet more items had come to light. These numbers form the basis of the numbers given to items of underglazed multicoloured printed wares throughout this book.

The first column gives the reference number as used in this book with H.G. Clarke's original numbers shown in brackets where applicable. The second column gives the title of the item of ware; the third column gives the number of engravings on the copper plates and column four the number of plates used. The final column is used for additional comments. An asterisk * against the title of a plate denotes that it was reissued by Cauldon.

Any variation from the details given in the final column denotes an earlier variety, e.g. No. 340, 'On Guard', shows a dog under the seat. This print, as with others which can show variations, must be a later copy; the earlier version shows a bucket under the seat, whereas this one replaces the bucket with a dog. Obviously, the plates must have been changed or reconditioned during the period of use. This means that any earlier or later copies can be recognised by reference to this Appendix.

Number		Title	Number of Engravings on Plate	Number of Plates	Comments
1	(1)	Alas! Poor Bruin	3	4	Lamp showing on sign.
4		Bear Hunting	2	4	With chequered and fancy border.
6	(6)	The Bear Pit	3	4	Complete with fancy border.
13	(12)	Shooting Bears	3	4	
19	(72)	Bear, Lion and Cock	3	4	Complete with fancy border.
25		Pegwell Bay, Est. 1760	2	4	
28		Bell Vue Tavern (with carriage)	1	4	
30		Bell Vue — Pegwell Bay	1	4	With bay window.
48	(123)	Pretty Kettle of Fish	2	4	With diamond shaped windows. No title.
49	(124)	Lobster Sauce	2	4	With square windows and no title. Shows marks on reverse where reconditioned.
53	(127)	Hauling in the Trawl	3	4	
54	(128)	Examining the Nets	1	5	The extra colour green.
350	(263)	Halt by the Wayside	1	5	All engraved on one plate.
443	(408)	The Milkmaid	1	5	
445	(444)	The Stall Woman	1	5	
54	(128A)	Examining the Nets	2	4	
55		Landing the Catch	2	4	
58	(135)	The Fishbarrow	3	4	
63	(142)	The Shrimpers	3	4	Adapted from two of Collins' paintings: 'The Prawn Fishers' and 'The Young Shrimpers'.

Number		Title	Number of Engravings on Plate	Number of Plates	Comments
71		Continental Fish Market.	1	4	Engraving to be used on a jar.
81		Meet of the Foxhounds	1	4	Engraving to be used on a jar.
96	(431)	Reception of H.R.H. Prince of Wales and Princess Alexandra 1863	1	4	Elongated print as used for a jar.
101	(38)	The Mirror	1	4	All engravings on one plate.
105	(33)	Lady Reading Book	1	4	
110	(32)	Lady Fastening Shoe	1	4	
102	(44)	The Toilette	3	4	With extra fancy border.
105	(33)	See No. 101			
106	(34)	Lady with Hawk	3	4	Complete with fancy border.
109	(30)	Lady, Boy and Mandoline	3	4	
110	(32)	See No. 101			
111	(31)	Lady Brushing Hair	1	4	Engraved on the reverse of the plate 'Jenny Lind'. All engravings on one plate.
118	(46)	Trysting Place	1	4	
119	(47)	The Lovers	1	4	
131/3			1	4	Different style of printing. No outline plate — replaced by green printing plate. All engravings on one plate.
131/4		Floral	1	4	
131/9		Subjects	1	4	
131/12A			1	4	
134	(51)	Exhibition Buildings 1851	2	4	Complete with acorn border.
134		Exhibition Buildings 1851	1	4	Similar print as above but with difference as noted when used for 'Princess Christian' vase. One engraving only on each plate except for outline plate which has, in addition, an outline engraving of flowers used on the reverse of the vase.
137	(55)	The Crystal Palace	2	4	Complete with border.
138	(56)	Interior View of Crystal Palace	2	4	
143	(61)	Dublin Industrial Exhibition 1853	2	4	Complete with fancy border.
145	(63)	L'Exposition Universelle de 1867	2	4	
147	(64)	Phildelphia Exhibition 1876	2	4	2 sets of oblong prints 3¾ ins., 4½ ins. 3 sets of round prints 4 ins., 4¾ ins., 5½ ins.
148	(65)	Paris Exhibition 1878	3	4	
149		England's Pride	2	4	Complete with fancy border.
153	(149)	The Late Prince Consort	3	4	With fancy border.
157	(150)	Albert Edward, Prince of Wales, and Princess Alexandra, on their Marriage 1863	3	4	Plate complete with outer Greek key border.
161	(95)	The Late Duke of Wellington	2	4	Shown with sash.
168	(70)	Allied Generals	2	4	Reg. mark incorporated in design.

Number		Title	Number of Engravings on Plate	Number of Plates	Comments
169		Garibaldi	3	4	
170	(155)	Sir Robert Peel	1	4	Name shown on book.
174	(153)	The Blue Boy	1	4	From Gainsborough's 'Blue Boy'.
248	(217)	Chiefs return from Deerstalking	1	4	From a painting by Landseer. Both engravings on one plate.
175		Dr. Johnson	3	4	Adapted from the painting by E.M. Ward 'Dr. Johnson in the ante-room of Lord Chesterfield'.
181	(161)	Sandringham	2	4	
185	(182)	St. Paul's Cathedral and River Pageant	2	4	There are two sizes of this plate — medium and large. Both plates have the title 'London' engraved on reverse.
188	(167)	Strathfieldsaye	2	4	
191	(168)	Albert Memorial	3	4	Engraved on reverse 'Made in England'. With carriage.
193	(172)	Charing Cross	3	4	Engraving on reverse 'Made in England'.
196	(171)	The New Blackfriars Bridge	3	4	
197	(183) (183A)	Thames Embankment	2	4	Each engraving shows different times, i.e. 1.30, 1.45 on clock. Engraved on reverse 'Made in England'.
198	(173)	Chapel Royal	2	4	
199		Choir of Chapel Royal, Savoy	2	4	
200	(170)	Alexandra Palace 1873	3	4	Oblong engraving.
201	(184)	Trafalgar Square	2	4	Adapted from Hawkins' painting 'Nelson Column'. Engraved on reverse 'Made in England'.
202	(176)	Holborn Viaduct	3	4	
203	(180)	New St. Thomas's Hospital	3	4	
205	(83)	The Thirsty Soldier	2	4	Adapted from a painting by F. Goodall 'The Tired Soldier'. No. 357 'The Irishman' is adapted from the same painting.
206		Embarking for the East	2	4	Complete with chain border.
209	(75)	Sebastopol	2	4	
210		The Battle of the Nile	3	4	
211	(80)	Meeting of Garibaldi and Victor Emmanuel	3	4	
212	(89)	War (after Wouvermann)	3	4	Both these prints adapted from Wouvermann's paintings.
213	(90)	Peace (after Wouvermann)	3	4	
218	(248)	Chin-Chew River	2	4	Marked 'Made in England' on reverse.
219	(87)	War	2	4	Adapted from Landseer's painting.
220		Peace	2	4	Adapted from Landseer's painting.
221	(264)	Harbour of Hong-Kong	2	4	Engraved on reverse 'Made in England'.
222	(278)	Ning Po River	2	4	

Number		Title	Number of Engravings on Plate	Number of Plates	Comments
223	(98)	Wimbledon July 1860	3	4	Date on plate as title.
224	(81)	Rifle Contest, Wimbledon 1864	2	4	
226	(188A)	Shakespeare's Birthplace (exterior)	2	4	Pearl dot border. Engraving on reverse 'Made in England'.
227	(189A)	Shakespeare's Birthplace (interior)	2	4	Pearl dot border. Engraving on reverse 'Made in England'.
228	(190A)	Ann Hathaway's Cottage	2	4	Pearl dot border. Engraving on reverse 'Made in England'.
229	(191)	Holy Trinity Church Stratford-on-Avon	2	4	Pearl dot border incorporated in engraving.
230	(192)	Seven Ages of Man	3	4	Line border.
231	(193)	Hamlet and his Father's Ghost	3	4	Line border.
232	(204)	The Village Wakes	2	4	With extra fancy border.
235		Il Penseroso*	3	4	From Webster's painting 'Il Penseroso'. Extra engraved mark on reverse 'No. 3'.
236	(201)	The Parish Beadle	2	4	Complete with outline border to be printed in black.
238	(206)	Xmas Eve	2	4	Complete with extra black border and registration mark.
239	(203)	The Swing*	2	4	
240	(205)	The Village Wedding*	3	4	From the painting by David Teniers. Extra mark 'No. 8' to Cauldon mark. No registration mark shown on engraving, obviously early plates reconditioned.
241		Our Home	2	4	Registration mark and J. Austin included in engraving.
242		Our Pets	2	4	Registration mark and J. Austin included in engraving.
245		The Enthusiast	3	4	From the painting by Theodore Lane.
246	(212)	Blind Man's Buff	3	4	
247	(224)	Master of the Hounds	3	4	
248		See No. 174			
249	(218)	Dangerous Skating	3	4	Extra border.
252		A Pair	3	4	
253		Snap Dragon	3	4	
254	(211)	The Best Card*	2	4	Complete with fancy border. Adapted from J. Burnett's 'The Best Card'.
255		Hide and Seek*	3	4	
256	(207)	A Fix*	2	4	From J. Burnett's picture 'Playing Draughts'. This engraving is with broom and tub. A similar engraving from the Mayer factory does not have these items.

Number		Title	Number of Engravings on Plate	Number of Plates	Comments
257	(210)	A Race or Derby Day	3	4	
258	(226)	The Skaters	3	4	
259	(223)	The Sportsman	3	4	
260	(220)	The Game Bag	3	4	Adapted from Lee's painting 'The Coverside'.
263	(216)	Children Sailing Boats in Tub	One of	4	Webster's Contrary Winds'.
270	(242)	The Begging Dog	each print	4	Landseer's 'The Beggar'.
316	(270)	Lady, Boy and Goats	all on one	4	Landseer's 'Harvest-time in the Highlands'.
341	(136)	The Fisher-Boy	plate	4	J.G. Naish's 'The Fisher Boy'.
264		Nine Dogs)	1	5	Marked 12 size jug.
264		Six Dogs)	1	5	
264		Six Dogs)	1	5	Marked 24 size jug.
264		Seven Dogs)	1	5	
264		Five Dogs)	1	5	Marked 30 size jug.
264		Eight Dogs)	1	5	
264		Nine Dogs)	1	5	
264		Four Dogs)	1	5	Marked 30-36 size mug.
264		Six Dogs)	1	5	
		Where bracketed the prints are engraved on one plate			The lower the size number, the larger the mug. In each instance the extra colour is damson.
265	(322)	Good Dog	3	4	Adapted from Landseer's painting 'The Friends'.
266		Contrast	3	4	
269	(238B)	Deerhound Guarding Cradle	1	4	All on one plate with extra fancy border. No.
309	(255)	The Faithful Shepherd	1	4	269 possibly adapted from Landseer's 'High
318	(280)	The Old Water-Mill	1	4	Life'.
270		See No. 263			
271		Pompey and Caesar	3	4	From Landseer's painting 'The Cavalier's Pets'.
272		Both Alike	3	4	
273	(228)	Country Quarters	3	4	
274		High Life	3	4	Adapted from a painting by Landseer.
275		Low Life	3	4	Adapted from a painting by Landseer.
276		The Snow-Drift	3	4	Adapted from Landseer's 'Highland Shepherd's Dog in the Snow'.
277	(238)	The Skewbald Horse	3	4	From a painting by P. Wouvermann.
278		The Robin	1	4	Both engravings on one plate.
286		Snowy Owl and Young	1	4	
279		A Pair of Wrens*	1	5	Both engravings on one plate. The extra colour
285		The Reed Warbler*	1	5	green.
281		The Cuckoo*	1	5	Both engravings on one plate. The extra colour
284		The Bullfinch and the Canary*	1	5	damson.
282		Blue Tit and Long-Tailed Tit*	1	5	Both engravings on one plate. The extra colour
293		The Thrush*	1	5	green.

Number		Title	Number of Engravings on Plate	Number of Plates	Comments
283		The Swallow	1	4	Blue plate missing. Both engravings on one
298		The Bullfinch	1	4	plate. The extra colour damson.
284		See No. 281			
285		See No. 279			
286		See No. 278			
287		The Kestrel*	1	5	The extra colour damson. Both engravings on
289		The Sea Eagle*	1	5	one plate.
288	(503)	The Buzzard	1	5	Both engravings on one plate. The extra colour
290	(502)	The Condor and the Snake	1	5	damson.
289		See No. 287			
290		See No. 288			
291		The Heron	1	5	The extra colour green.
292	(501)	Eagle Owl and Merlin	1	5	The extra colour damson.
293		See No. 282			
294		The Chaffinch	1	5	Both engravings on one plate. The extra colour
300		The Nightingale	1	5	green.
298		See No. 283			
300		See No. 294			
304	(508)	The Storm Petrel*	1	5	An extra engraved mark on reverse 'Ridg-
305	(507)	Red-Backed Shrike*	1	5	wood'. Damson the extra colour. These four
306	(506)	Lesser-Spotted Woodpecker*	1	5	engraved prints on one plate.
307	(505)	The Owl*	1	5	
308	(253)	Dutch Winter Scene	3	3	
309		See No. 269			
310	(265)	H.R.H. the Prince of Wales Visiting the Tomb of Washington	3	4	
311	(267)	I See You, My Boy	2	4	With narrow leaf border.
312	(239)	French Street Scene	2	4	Two complete sets of plates, 4ins., 4¾ins.
313	(250)	Cottage Children	1	4	Adapted from Gainsborough's painting 'The Cottage Children'.
315	(246)	Cattle and Ruins	2	4	Complete with fancy border.
316		See No. 263			
317		Lend a Bite	3	4	From Mulready's painting 'Lending a Bite'.
318		See No. 269			
319	(512)	The Queen God Bless Her	2	4	With extra fancy border.
321	(251)	Deer Drinking	3	4	
322		The Rivals	3	4	
323	(252)	The Dentist	1	4	From a painting by Isach Van Ostade.
324	(254)	The Farriers	2	4	Adapted from Wouvermann's 'The Smithy'.
327		The Times	3	4	From a painting by Goode 'The Newspaper'.

Number		Title	Number of Engravings on Plate	Number of Plates	Comments
328		Uncle Toby	3	4	From the painting by C.R. Leslie 'Uncle Toby and the Widow'.
329	(257)	The First Appeal	2	4	Adapted from F. Stone's painting 'The Last Appeal'. Border complete with print.
330	(258)	The Second Appeal	2	4	Adapted from the painting 'The Last Appeal' by F. Stone. Complete with border.
332	(303)	Transplanting Rice	2	4	
333	(306)	Vue de la Ville de Strasbourg Pris du Port	2	4	Complete with fancy border. 2 complete sets, 4ins., 5ins.
334	(84)	The Trooper*	3	4	From a painting by Herring, Bright and Baxter. 'No. 12' engraved as an extra mark to Cauldon.
335	(259)	Fording the Stream*	3	4	'No. 5' engraved extra to Cauldon mark.
338	(262)	Grace Before Meals	2	4	Outline in black.
340		On Guard*	3	4	'No. 4' engraved plus Cauldon mark. Dog under seat.
341		See No. 263			
343	(275)	The Maidservant	3	4	
344	(277)	Negro with Pitcher	1	5	The Quarry is adapted from Wouvermann's picture 'Landscape'. Both engravings on one plate.
352	(286)	The Quarry	1	5	
345	(261)	Girl with Grapes	1	4	With engraved stamp on reverse 'J. Gosnell & Co. London'. Both engravings on one plate.
348	(281)	Peasant Boys	1	4	
350		See No. 54			
351	(285)	Preparing for the Ride	3	4	From a painting by Mourenhout 'Preparing for the Chase.
352		See No. 344			
354	(283)	The Picnic	2	4	
356	(238A)	The Cavalier*	3	4	Adapted from the painting by Herring, Bright and Baxter, who also painted No. 334, 'The Trooper'.
358	(273)	Little Red-Riding Hood	3	4	
359	(288)	The Red Bull Inn*	2	4	Extra fancy border. 'No. 6' engraved plus Cauldon mark. No name over door.
360	(240)	Letter from the Diggings	2	4	Possibly adapted from the Baxter print 'News from Australia'.
363		The Listener	2	4	'J. Gosnell & Co. London' stamp engraved on reverse. J. Austin engraved on print.
364	(297)	The Strawberry Girl	2	4	From 'The Strawberry Girl' by Reynolds.
365		The Waterfall	2	4	
369		Fisherman's Abode	1	4	All four engravings on one plate. Very small size.
370		The Round Tower	1	4	
371		Monastic Ruins	1	4	
373		Ruined Temples	1	4	

Number		Title	Number of Engravings on Plate	Number of Plates	Comments
372	(294)	The Shrine	1	4	All three engravings on one plate.
376	(290)	Ruined Abbey Chancel	1	4	
377	(299)	Watering Cattle	1	4	
382		The Cattle Drover		5	Green the extra colour.
398		Village Scene on the Continent	All on	5	
399		The Windmill	one	5	
407		View near St. Michael's Mount	plate	5	
383	(313)	Continental Scene	1	4	All engravings on one plate.
389	(318)	The Ferry Boat	1	4	
394	(328)	The Stone Bridge	1	4	
433	(384)	Grecian Landscape	1	4	
384		The Deer-Stalker	1	5	From Landseer's paintings 'On the Look-out' and 'The Alarm'. The extra colour green.
385		Wild Deer	1	5	
386		The Donkey's Foal	1	4	No. 386 adapted from Park's painting 'From the Moors', No. 391 from Le Poittevin's 'The Studio of Paul Potter'. All four engravings on one plate.
391		Milking the Cow	1	4	
393		A Sea-Shore Study	1	4	
397		Tyrolese Village Scene	1	4	
388		Cows in Stream Near Ruins	1	5	All engravings on one plate. The extra colour green.
390		Halt Near Ruins	1	5	
400		The Wooden Bridge	1	5	
403		Horse drawing Boat	1	5	
388	(314)	Cows in Stream Near Ruins	1	5	Both engravings on one plate. The extra colour green.
428	(439)	A Rural Scene	1	5	
389		See No. 383			
390		See No. 388			
391		See No. 386			
393		See No. 386			
394		See No. 383			
395		The Stone Jetty	1	5	All on one plate. The extra colour green.
396		The Travellers' Departure	1	5	
411		The Torrent	1	5	
397		Tyrolese Village Scene (see also No. 386)	1	4	Both engravings on one plate.
409		Bridge across the Gap	1	4	
398		See No. 382			
399		See No. 382			
400		See No. 388			
401		Uncle Tom and Eva	1	4	Both engravings on one plate.
402		Uncle Tom	1	4	
403		See No. 388			
404		Passing the Pipe	1	4	Both engravings on one plate.
405		The Smokers	1	4	
407		See No. 382			
409		See No. 397			

Number		Title	Number of Engravings on Plate	Number of Plates	Comments
411		See No. 395			
412	(271)	The Last In*	1	4	From Mulready's 'The Last In'.
413	(304)	The Truant*	1	5	Adapted from T. Webster's 'Going to School'. Damson the extra colour.
414		The Hop Queen	1	4	Adapted from Withrington's 'Crown of Hops'. Extra mark engraved on reverse '28/12/51'.
415	(352)	The Bully	1	5	Damson the extra colour. Outline plate in black.
416	(396)	Landscape and River Scene	1	5	Adapted from H. Gastineau's 'Llangollen, Denbighshire'. These plates have the name 'Llangollen' engraved on the reverse. Extra colour damson.
418		Highland Music	1	4	From Landseer's 'Highland Music'.
420		Roman Ruins	1	4	Both engravings on one plate.
421		The Ruined Temple	1	4	
423		The Mountain Stream	1	5	Adapted from H. Gastineau's 'View of the Vale of Llangollen'. The extra colour damson.
428		See No. 388			
430		Tremadoc	1	5	Both engravings on one plate. Extra colour damson.
435		Haddon Hall	1	5	
432	(460)	The Two Anglers	1	5	Adapted from H. Gastineau's 'View of the Vale of Llangollen' showing Crow Castle. Extra colour damson.
435		Haddon Hall	1	5	Both engravings on one plate. The extra colour damson.
437		Chatsworth	1	5	
440		Chinese River Scene with Junks	1	5	From the painting by T. Allom 'Golden Island' — Yangtse River. The extra colour used is damson.
443		See No. 54			
444A	(390)	Independence Hall Philadelphia (interior view)	2	4	Engraved on reverse 'Kerr's China Hall is opposite the above'. Obviously meant to be printed under picture.
444B	(445)	State House in Philadelphia 1776	1	4	Engraved on reverse 'R.T. Allen, Son & Co., 309/311 Market Street, Philadelphia'. Also 'F. & R. Pratt & Co., Fenton, Staffordshire'.
445		See No. 54			
448		Ecclesiastical Subjects	1	5	From a drawing by Copley Fielding 'Chepstow Castle'.
		Two Fish in Stream	1	5	This plate does not appear in any records. The extra colour green.

APPENDIX II

THE BOOK OF FACTORY PULLS
AS USED BYTHE PRATT/CAULDON COMBINE

In addition to the information on the copper plates (see Appendix I), it is now possible to give details from the actual book of factory 'pulls' as used by Cauldon until cessation.

This book shows the combined engravings from both the Pratt and Cauldon factories which remove any doubt at all of the origin of the titles shown. These pulls from the original outline copper plate show the subject in detail and were used as a reference between customer and factory whenever orders were placed.

No.	Title	No.	Title
1	Alas! Poor Bruin	147	Philadelphia Exhibition 1876 (2 varieties, oblong)
4	Bear Hunting		
6	The Bear Pit	147	Philadelphia Exhibition 1876 (2 varieties, circular)
9	Bears at School		
13	Shooting Bears	148	Paris Exhibition 1878
19	Bear, Lion and Cock	149	England's Pride
25	Pegwell Bay, Est. 1760	153	The Late Prince Consort
28	Belle Vue Tavern (with carriage)	157	Albert Edward, Prince of Wales, and Princess Alexandra, on their Marriage in 1863
30	Belle Vue — Pegwell Bay		
48	Pretty Kettle of Fish	161	The Late Duke of Wellington
49	Lobster Sauce	168	Allied Generals
53	Hauling in the Trawl	169	Garibaldi
54	Examining the Nets (2 varieties)	170	Sir Robert Peel
55	Landing the Catch	175	Dr. Johnson
58	The Fishbarrow	181	Sandringham
60	The Net Mender	185	St. Paul's Cathedral and River Pageant (2 varieties)
62	Foreign River Scene		
63	The Shrimpers	188	Strathfieldsaye
66	Dutch River Scene	191	Albert Memorial
71	Continental Fish Market	193	Charing Cross
81	Meet of the Foxhounds	196	The New Blackfriars Bridge
96	Reception of H.R.H. Prince of Wales and Princess Alexandra 1863	197	Thames Embankment
		198	Chapel Royal
102	The Toilette	199	Choir of Chapel Royal, Savoy
105	Lady Reading Book	201	Trafalgar Square
106	Lady with Hawk	202	Holborn Viaduct
109	Lady, Boy and Mandoline	203	New St. Thomas's Hospital
111	Lady Brushing Hair	205	Thirsty Soldier
113	Fruit and Statue Piece	206	Embarking for the East
118	The Trysting Place	209	Sebastopol
119	The Lovers	210	The Battle of the Nile
131/3)		211	Meeting of Garibaldi and Victor Emmanuel
131/9)		212	War (after Wouvermann)
131/12A)		213	Peace (after Wouvermann)
131/13)		218	Chin-Chew River
131/15)		219	War
131/17)	Floral Subjects	220	Peace
131/20)		221	Harbour of Hong-Kong
131/21)		222	Ning Po River
131/22)		223	Wimbledon July 1860
131/24)		224	Rifle Contest, Wimbledon 1864
131/34)		226	Shakespeare's Birthplace (exterior)
Plus five which cannot be deciphered due to poor printing.		227	Shakespeare's Birthplace (interior)
134	Exhibition Buildings 1851 (2 varieties)	228	Ann Hathaway's Cottage
		229	Holy Trinity Church, Stratford-on-Avon
137	The Crystal Palace	230	Seven Ages of Mann
138	Interior View of Crystal Palace	231	Hamlet and His Father's Ghost
143	Dublin Industrial Exhibition 1853	232	The Village Wakes
145	L'Exposition Universelle de 1867		

No.	Title	No.	Title
235	Il Penseroso	311	I See You, My Boy
236	The Parish Beadle	312	French Street Scene (2 varieties)
238	Xmas Eve	313	Cottage Children
239	The Swing	315	Cattle and Ruins
240	The Village Wedding	316	Lady, Boy and Goats
241	Our Home	317	Lend a Bite
242	Our Pets	319	The Queen, God Bless Her
245	The Enthusiast	321	Deer Drinking
246	Blind Man's Buff	322	The Rivals
247	Master of the Hounds	323	The Dentist
249	Dangerous Skating	324	The Farriers
252	A Pair	327	The Times
253	Snap Dragon	328	Uncle Toby
254	The Best Card	329C	The First Appeal (3rd issue)
255	Hide and Seek	330	The Second Appeal (3rd issue)
256	The Fix	332	Transplanting Rice
257	A Race or Derby Day	333	Vue de la Ville de Strasbourg, Pris du Port
258	The Skaters		(2 varieties)
260	The Game Bag	334	The Trooper
263	Children Sailing Boat in Rub	335	Fording the Stream
264(a)	Four Dogs	338	Grace Before Meals
264(b)	Five Dogs	340	On Guard
264(c)	Six Dogs (3 varieties)	341	The Fisher-Boy
264(d)	Seven Dogs	343	The Maidservant
264(e)	Eight Dogs	344	Negro with Pitcher
264(f)	Nine Dogs (2 varieties)	348	Peasant Boys
265	Good Dog	349	The Poultry Woman
266	Contrast	350	Halt by the Wayside
270	Begging Dog	351	Preparing for the Ride
271	Pompey and Caesar	352	The Quarry
272	Both Alike	353	Persuasion
273	Country Quarters	354	The Picnic
274	High Life	356	The Cavalier
275	Low Life	358	Little Red-Riding Hood
276	The Snow-Drift	359	Red Bull Inn (extra border — no name)
277	The Skewbald Horse	360	Letter from the Diggings
278	The Robin	361	The Wolf and the Lamb
279	A Pair of Wrens	363	The Listener
280	The Goldfinch	364	The Strawberry Girl
281	The Cuckoo	365	The Waterfall
282	Blue Tit and Long-Tailed Tit	369	Fisherman's Abode
283	The Swallow	370	The Round Tower
284	The Bullfinch and the Canary	371	Monastic Ruins
285	The Reed Warbler	372	The Shrine
286	Snowy Owl and Young	373	Ruined Temples
287	The Kestrel	375	The Toll Bridge
288	The Buzzard	376	Ruined Abbey Chancel
289	The Sea Eagle	377	Watering Cattle
290	The Condor and the Snake	378	The Crooked Bridge
291	The Heron	383	Continental Scene
292	Eagle Owl and Merlin	384	The Deer-Stalker
293	The Thrush	385	Wild Deer
294	The Chaffinch	386	The Donkey's Foal
300	The Nightingale	388	Cows in Stream near Ruins
304	The Storm Petrel	389	The Ferry Boat
305	Red-Backed Shrike	390	Halt Near Ruins
306	Lesser-Spotted Woodpecker	391	Milking the Cow
307	The Owl	393	A Sea-Shore Study
308	Dutch Winter Scene	394	The Stone Bridge
309	The Faithful Shepherd	395	The Stone Jetty
310	H.R.H. Prince of Wales Visiting the Tomb of	396	The Travellers' Departure
	Washington	398	Village Scene on the Continent

No.	Title	No.	Title
399	The Windmill	422	The Rustic Laundrywoman
400	The Wooden Bridge	423	Mountain Stream
401	Uncle Tom and Eva	430	Tremadoc
402	Uncle Tom	432	The Two Anglers
403	Horses Drawing Boat	433	Grecian Landscape
404	Passing the Pipe	435	Haddon Hall (2 varieties)
405	The Smokers	436	Hafod
407	View near St. Michael's Mount	437	Chatsworth (2 varieties)
409	Bridge across the Gap	440	Chinese River Scene with Junks
410	Tyrolese Hill Scene	441	Roman Ruins and Pedestrians
411	The Torrent	443	The Milkmaid
412	The Last In	444	Philadelphia Public Buildings 1876
413	The Truant	444A	Interior View, Independence Hall, Philadelphia
415	The Bully	444B	State House in Philadelphia 1776
416	Landscape and River Scene	444C	Philadelphia Exhibition 1876 (similar to No. 147 circular print)
418	Highland Music	445	The Stall Woman
420	Roman Ruins	448	Ecclesiastical Subjects
421	The Ruined Temple		

APPENDIX III

WARES PRODUCED BY MAYERS

(Items known to have been reissued by Kirkhams c.1920 are marked with an asterisk *)

No.	Title	No.	Title
3	Bear's Grease Manufacturer	140	Opening Ceremony 1851 Exhibition
10	Bears on Rock	141	Closing Ceremony 1851 Exhibition
24	Pegwell Bay, Lobster Fishing	142*	New York 1853
32	Pegwell Bay, S. Banger, Shrimp Sauce Manufacturer	150	Queen Victoria on Balcony
34	The Dutch Fisherman	155	Edward VII and Queen Alexandra
35	Pegwell Bay, Ramsgate (Still-life Game)	158	Wellington (Cocked Hat)
36	Pegwell Bay, Ramsgate (Still-life Fish)	160A	Wellington (Clasped Hands)
37	Pegwell Bay, Ramsgate (Farmyard Scene)	163*	Wellington (Funeral)
44	Sandown Castle, Kent	164	Tria Juncta in Uno
46	Walmer Castle (with sentry)	165	Alma
47	Walmer Castle (without horses)	166	Balaklava, Inkerman, Alma
50*	Injury	167	Sir Charles Napier
51*	Revenge	172	Harriett Beecher Stowe
52	Shells (various)	176*	Buckingham Palace
56	Mending the Nets	178	Windsor Castle or Prince Albert (Hare Coursing)
57*	The Fishmarket	179*	Drayton Manor
69	Pegwell Bay, Kent (jar)	182*	Osborne House
72	The Fleet at Anchor (jar)	183*	New Houses of Parliament (large size)
73	Landing of the British Army at the Crimea (jar)	190	Albert Memorial (without carriage)
74	Battle of Alma (with date) (jar)	192A	St. Paul's Cathedral (without 'Entered Stationers' Hall')
75	Battle of Alma (without date) (jar)	194	Eleanor Cross
76	Charge of Scots Greys at Balaklava (jar)	216	The Redoubt
77	The Dragoon Charge — Balaklava (jar)	217*	Conway Castle
78	The Fall of Sebastopol (jar)	244*	The Bull Fight
79	Sir Harry Jones (jar)	251*	A False Move
83	The Chalees Satoon (jar)	256*	A Fix (without Broom and Tub)
84	Venice (jar)	261*	Pheasant Shooting
96D	Exterior View, 1851 Exhibition (extra large size)	262*	The Boar Hunt
97	The Bride	296	The Kingfisher
98	An Eastern Repast	314	Breakfast Party
99	Eastern Lady Dressing Hair	331	Strasbourg
104	Reflection in Mirror	342*	Summer (plaque)
117	The Tryst	342A*	Autumn
131	Flowers (various)	342B	Spring (plaque)
131/8	Floral (Old World Garden)	366*	Youth and Age
135	Exterior 1851 Exhibition	380A	Maidens Decorating Bust of Homer
136	Interior 1851 Exhibition (without fountain)	380	The Music Lesson
139	Interior 1851 Exhibition (with fountain)		

The items marked with asterisks are not necessarily the full list of reissues, but those known to the author. Note: No jars have ever been seen as reissues, except the one from the Pratt/Cauldon combine, 'The Reception of H.R.H. Prince of Wales and Princess Alexandra at London Bridge 7th March 1863'.

APPENDIX IV
POT-LIDS BASED ON CONTEMPORARY PAINTINGS AND PRINTS

No.	Title	Title of Painting	Painted By	Details From
2	Bear attacked by Dogs		F. Snyders	*Masterpieces of Celebrated Painters*, 1858.
13	Shooting Bears	Bear Hunt in the Pyrenees		*Illustrated London News*, January 29th, 1853.
25	Pegwell Bay Established 1760		Sir Frank Short RA	Original in Harewood House.
34	The Dutch Fisherman	Shakespeare's Cliff, Dover, Kent	H. Gastineau	Freely adapted from *Picturesque Beauties of Great Britain*, published 1828.
37	Pegwell Bay, Ramsgate (Farmyard Scene)	The Farm-yard	T.S. Cooper	Adapted freely from the painting as seen in the *Art Journal* of 1852.
39	New Jetty and Pier, Margate	The New Landing Place and Pier from the Port, Margate	Possibly W.H. Bartlett	Early 19th century print, possibly from the *Watering Places of Great Britain and Fashionable Directory*, published c.1835.
41	Royal Harbour, Ramsgate		W.H. Bartlett	Frontispiece to above.
53	Hauling in the Trawl	Herring Fishing Isle-of-Man	E.D. Engraved by Linton	From a drawing published in *Illustrated London News*, 6th March 1847.
58	The Fishbarrow		Jan Steen	1927 Pot-Lid Book.
63	The Shrimpers	The Prawn Fishers The Young Shrimpers	W. Collins RA	*Art Journal*, 1849 *Art Journal*, 1857.
83	The Chalees Satoon	The Chalees Satoon East India	W. Daniell RA	*The Picture Printer*, by C. Lewis.
84	Venice			*Le Blond Book*, by C. Lewis.
89	The Stone Jetty	The Homeward Bound	F.R. Lee RA	Art Union 1848. See No. 395.
100	Eastern Lady and Black Attendant			Kronheim print.
102	The Toilette	Interior of Dutch House, latter half of 17th century	Casper Netscher	*Chats on Old Furniture*, by Arthur Hayden.
103	The Packman		J. Nash	*Kenilworth*, by Sir Walter Scott.
112	The Spanish Lady	The Bull-fight	G. Herbert	Pot-Lid Circle Data-sheet No. 8.
124	Bay of Naples	Bay of Naples Early Morning	W. Gallow	*Art Journal*, 1856.
133	Grand International Buildings of 1851	Great Exhibition Polka 1851		*Victoria's Heyday*, by J.B. Priestley.
140	The Great Exhibition of 1851 (Opening Ceremony)		Eugene Lamé	*Life and Times of Queen Victoria*.
141	Great Exhibition of 1851 (Closing Ceremony)		W. Simpson	*Centenary Pot-Lid Book*.

No.	Title	Title of Painting	Painted By	Details From
150	Queen Victoria on Balcony	Baptism of the Prince of Wales in St. George's Chapel, Windsor	Sir George Hayter	*The Picture Printer*, by C. Lewis.
154	Queen Victoria and Albert Edward		R. Thorburn	*Centenary Pot-Lid Book.*
161	The Late Duke of Wellington		Count D'Orsay	*Age of Paradox*, by John W. Dodds.
163	Funeral of the late Duke of Wellington			*The Picture Printer*, by C. Lewis.
174	The Blue Boy		T. Gainsborough RA	*Masterpieces of Celebrated Painters*, 1858.
175	Dr. Johnson	Dr. Johnson in the Anteroom of Lord Chesterfield	E.M. Ward ARA	*Art Journal*, 1853.
180	Windsor Park (Returning from Stag-Hunting)			*The Picture Printer*, by C. Lewis.
182	Osborne House			*Le Blond print.*
201	Trafalgar Square	The Nelson Column	G. Hawkins	*Art Journal*, 1850.
205	The Thirsty Soldier	The Tired Soldier	F. Goodall	*Art Journal*, 1852. (see No. 357).
212	War		Wouvermann	*Centenary Pot-Lid Book.*
213	Peace		Wouvermann	*Centenary Pot-Lid Book.*
217	Conway Castle		H. Gastineau	*Wales Illustrated*, a series of views published 1830.
219	War		Sir Edwin Landseer RA	*Art Journal*, 1854.
220	Peace		Sir Edwin Landseer RA	*Art Journal*, 1854.
223	Wimbledon 1860		A. Maclure	1927 Pot-Lid Book.
233	May Day Dancers at the Swan Inn	May Day		*Le Blond Book*, 1920.
234	Pet Rabbits	The Pet Rabbits		*Le Blond Book*, 1920.
235	Il Penseroso		T. Webster RA	*Centenary Pot-Lid Book.*
236	Parish Beadle	The Parish Beadle	D. Wilkie RA	*Centenary Pot-Lid Book.*
240	The Village Wedding		D. Teniers	*Centenary Pot-Lid Book.*
243	The Buffalo Hunt	An Indian Buffalo Hunt	G. Catlin	*Centenary Pot-Lid Book.*
244	The Bull Fight	Bull Fight Seville	Lake Price or G. Herbert	*Maps and Prints for Pleasure and Investment.*
245	The Enthusiast		T. Lane	*Art Journal*, 1850.
247	Master of Hounds	Drawn Blank	H. Hall	Pot-Lid Circle Data Sheet No. 31.
248	Chiefs Return from Deerstalking		Sir Edwin Landseer RA	*Centenary Pot-Lid Book.* It has been suggested that R. Ansdell RA painted this picture but as it was exhibited in 1827 when Ansdell was only twelve, no doubt Ansdell later painted a copy.
253	Snap Dragon			Victorian music cover. (Snap Dragon Polka).
254	The Best Card		J. Burnett	*Centenary Pot-Lid Book.*

No.	Title	Title of Painting	Painted By	Details From
255	Hide and Seek		R.T. Ross RSA	*Art Journal,* 1871. This painting was previously credited to T. Faed RA.
256	A Fix	Playing Draughts	J. Burnett	*Centenary Pot-Lid Book.*
258	The Skaters	The Winter Season	Unknown	Victorian music sheet cover.
260	The Game Dog	The Cover Side	F.R. Lee RA	*Art Journal,* 1851. Landseer sketched in the figures of the gamekeepers and the dogs.
263	Children Sailing Boat in Tub	Contrary Winds	T. Webster RA	*Art Journal,* 1875.
264	Dogs	Highland Dogs	Sir Edwin Landseer RA	*Country Life Annual,* 1962.
265	Good Dog	The Friends	Sir Edwin Landseer RA	*Art Journal,* 1861. This lid is in reverse to the painting.
269	Fidelity or Deerhound guarding Cradle	High Life	Sir Edwin Landseer RA	Possibly adapted from the painting of 'High Life'. The dog is a carbon copy.
270	The Begging Dog	The Beggar	Sir Edwin Landseer RA	*Art Journal,* 1876. This is a drawing signed and dated 1824, which was sold in the sale of Landseer's effects.
271	Pompey and Caesar	The Cavalier's Pets	Sir Edwin Landseer RA	*Art Journal,* 1852.
272	Both Alike	The Breakfast	Sir Edwin Landseer RA	Art Union 1848.
273	Country Quarters		A. Adams	Original in a collection on the Continent.
274	High Life		Sir Edwin Landseer RA	*Art Journal,* 1849.
275	Low Life		Sir Edwin Landseer RA	*Art Journal,* 1849.
276	The Snowdrift	Highland Shepherd Dog in Snow	Sir Edwin Landseer RA	*Art Journal,* 1875. The title is the one which Landseer gave this painting when exhibited in 1834. Engravings of a later date have the titles 'The Rescue' and 'The Snowdrift'.
277	The Skewbald Horse		P. Wouvermann	*Centenary Pot-Lid Book.*
309	Faithful Shepherd		Nicholas Berghem	*Masterpieces of Celebrated Painters,* 1858.
311	I See You, My Boy		Girardet	A Victorian engraving. (Both this and No. 363 were engraved by A.H. Payne of Dresden and Leipzig.)
313	The Cottage Children	Cottage Children	T. Gainsborough RA	*Art Journal,* 1850. This painting is often referred to as 'Rustic Children'.
316	Lady, Boy and Goats	Harvest Time in the Scottish Highlands	Sir Edwin Landseer RA and Sir A.W. Callcott	*Art Journal,* 1876. Figures by Landseer and landscape by Callcott.
317	Lend a Bite	Lending a Bite	W. Mulready RA	*Art Journal,* 1864. Exhibited in 1836.
318	The Old Watermill	Travellers Conversing	Nicholas Berghem	*Masterpieces of Celebrated Painters,* 1858.
319	The Queen, God Bless Her	Happy as a King	W. Collins RA	
323	The Dentist	L'Arracheur de dents (the tooth extractor)	Adrian van Ostade	*Bryan's Dictionary of Painters and Engravers,* Vol. 4, 1926.

No.	Title	Title of Painting	Painted By	Details From
324	The Farriers	The Smithy	P. Wouvermann	*Centenary Pot-Lid Book.*
327	The Times	The Newspaper	T.S. Good	*Art Journal*, 1852.
328	Uncle Toby	Uncle Toby and The Widow	C.R. Leslie RA	*Art Journal*, 1853. Uncle Toby is a portriat of Bannister, a celebrated comedian of the period, in a scene from *Tristram Shandy*. The painting was exhibited in 1831.
329	The First Appeal		F. Stone	*Centenary Pot-Lid Book.*
330	The Second Appeal	The Last Appeal	F. Stone	*Centenary Pot-Lid Book.*
334	The Trooper		Herring, Baxter and Bright	Art Journal, 1866. A composite effort, horses and dogs by Herring, figures by Baxter and landscape by Bright.
337	The Flute Player		Nicholas Lancret	*Centenary Pot-Lid Book.*
338	Grace Before Meals	Saying Grace	Jan Steem	*Connoisseur*, 1908.
341	The Fisher Boy		J.G. Naish	*Art Journal*, 1875.
345	Girl with Grapes	Sharing the Gains	B.E. Murillo	1924 Pot-Lid Book.
346	Tam-o-Shanter and Souter Johnny		Thomas	*Art Journal*, 1858.
347	Tam-o-Shanter		Thomas	*Art Journal*, 1858.
348	Peasant Boys	The Beggar Boys	B.E. Murillo	*The Penny Magazine*, 1841.
349	The Poultry Woman		C. Matzee	The original painting shows a nun in the archway.
351	Preparing for the Ride	Preparing for the Chase	Mourenhout	*Art Journal*, 1857.
352	The Quarry	Landscape	Wouvermann	*Pictorial Half Hours*, c.1840.
356	The Cavalier		Herring, Baxter and Bright	Details as for No. 334, 'The Trooper'.
357	The Irishman	The Tired Soldier	F. Goodall	*Art Journal*, 1852. (see No. 205.
361A	How I love to Laugh			*Pleasures of Human Life*, by Rowlandson.
363	The Listener	'Trina'	Meyerheim	A Victorian Engraving (see No. 311).
364	Strawberry Girl		Sir Joshua Reynolds RA	*Centenary Pot-Lid Book.*
375	The Toll Bridge	Pontypryd	H. Gastineau	*Wales Illustrated*, published 1830.
378	The Crooked Bridge	St. Goar on the Rhine	Brandard	Victorian sheet music covers.
384	The Deer Stalker	On the Lookout	Sir Edwin Landseer RA	*Art Journal*, 1875.
385	Wild Deer	The Alarm	Sir Edwin Landseer RA	*Art Journal*, 1876.
386	The Donkey's Foal	From the Moors	Park	*Art Journal*, 1859.
391	Milking the Cow	The Studio of Paul Potter	Le Poittevin	Art Union 1847.
393	A Sea-shore Study	Unknown	Stothard	One of the paintings by this artist used to illustrate Roger's *Italy,* 1830.
395	The Stone Jetty	The Homeward Bound	F.R. Lee RA	Art Union 1848 (see No. 89).
396	Travellers Departure	Starting for a Ride	A. Cuyp	*Masterpieces of Celebrated Painters,* 1858.

No.	Title	Title of Painting	Painted By	Details From
398	Village Scene on the Continent	Val St. Nicola	J.D. Harding	Pictorial Gallery of Arts.
400	The Wooden Bridge	Unknown	T. Packer	*Victorian Sheet Music Covers,* by D. Pearsall. The lid is in reverse to the drawing.
407	View near St. Michael's Mount	St. Michael's Mount	Clarkson Stanfield	1927 Pot-Lid Book.
411	The Torrent	Le Torrent	Berghem	1924 Pot-Lid Book.
412	The Last In		W. Mulready	*Art Journal,* 1850. Painted in 1835.
413	The Truant	Going to School	T. Webster	*Art Journal,* 1849. Exhibited in 1836.
414	The Hop Queen	Crown of Hops	W.F. Withrington	*Art Journal,* 1851. Exhibited in 1843.
415	The Bully	The Wolf and The Lamb	W. Mulready	*Art Journal,* 1856.
416	Landscape and River Scene	Llangollen, Denbighshire	H. Gastineau	*Wales Illustrated,* 1830.
417	The Blind Fiddler		Sir David Wilkie RA	*Centenary Pot-Lid Book.*
418	Highland Music		Sir Edwin Landseer RA	*Art Journal,* 1849. Painted in 1832 but never exhibited. Sold direct to Mr. Vernon.
419	The Travelling Knife-Grinder	The Knife-Grinder	D. Teniers	*Penny Magazine,* 1834 (see No. 451).
422	The Rustic Laundry-woman		Nicholas Berghem	National Picture Print Society Vol. 1.
423	Mountain Stream	View of the Vale of Llangollen	H. Gastineau	*Wales Illustrated, 1830.*
424	Christ in the Cornfield		H. Warren	*Centenary Pot-Lid Book.*
428	A Rural Scene	The Knife-Grinder	D. Teniers	*Penny Magazine,* 1834 (see No. 419).
431	The Spanish Dancers	Fêtes Venitiennes	Antoine Watteau	National Gallery of Scotland.
432	The Two Anglers	View of the Vale of Llangollen with Crow Castle	C. Marshall	*Exchange and Mart,* 1937.
440	Chinese River Scene with Junks	Golden Island Yangtse River	T. Allom	G. Godden.
448	Ecclesiastical Subjects	View near Aber	H. Gastineau	*Wales Illustrated,* published 1830.

APPENDIX V
HISTORICAL NOTES

Nos. 74 and 75 Battle of the Alma
The Crimean War
On September 19th, 1854, a force of 25,000 English, 25,000 French and 8,000 Turkish soldiers began a combined advance on Sebastopol and, on the 20th September, encountered the Russian forces under the command of Prince Menschikoff, who were strongly entrenched on the heights south of the River Alma.

Prince Menschikoff had allowed all the invading troops to disembark in safety, thinking that his position was impregnable and the allied armies were entering a trap, but, at two o'clock on September 20th, the allies crossed the Alma under very heavy fire and advanced up the opposing slopes where the Russian batteries were situated. After two hours of very heavy fighting, including hand to hand combat, the position was taken, but not without very heavy losses, the English losing 2,000, including 26 officers, whilst the French also lost 1,200 troops.

No. 76 Charge of the Scots Greys at Balaklava
No. 77 The Dragoon Charge — Balaklava
The Crimean War
On October 25th 1854, General Liprandi, the Russian commander, attacked the English camp at Balaklava, with approximately 25,000 men under his command.

This is the day which is forever destined to be remembered for the disastrous Charge of the Light Brigade. The Russians, in the initial stages, captured four posts held by Turkish forces and followed up this success by attacking the English position with 3,000 cavalry, but the Scots Greys and the Enniskillens, although hopelessly outnumbered, charged on either flank and the Russians were compelled to retreat. This action was completed in only five minutes.

These combined Scots Greys and Enniskillens were known as 'The Heavy Brigade' and this was the position when Lord Raglan gave an order to Lord Lucan — ''Prevent the enemy from taking away their guns''. This seemed an impossible task; the battery of eight Russian guns were at the end of the valley and supported on each flank by artillery.

Lord Lucan hesitated to carry out this order, but the order was explicit, so he directed Lord Cardigan to form his 'Light Brigade', composed of the 13th Light Lancers and the 17th Lancers in one line, with the 4th Light Dragoons and the 11th Hussars in the second. The command to charge was given and 673 men rode down that valley to charge the guns.

As history records, this charge was a total failure and only 195 men returned from 'The charge of the Light Brigade'.

No. 116 Jenny Lind
Several stories concerning her life in England are told of the Swedish singer whose voice enthralled all who heard her. Two connect her with Queen Victoria.

It is stated that, shortly after the arrival of Jenny Lind in England, Queen Victoria sent an invitation for her to sing at Buckingham Palace. Unfortunately, Jenny Lind had a contract which forbade her to sing anywhere but at the Italian Opera House. Therefore, she sent her regrets and turned down the invitation. This action so much upset Jenny Lind that, very impetuously, she set out for Buckingham Palace to explain her reasons in person. Her arrival at the Palace caused a great deal of commotion and she refused to accept any denial of seeing the Queen. Eventually, she persuaded someone in authority to take her card to the Queen and, through her persistence, was able to make her apologies personally.

On another occasion, when giving a private concert before the Queen, Jenny Lind noticed that the pianist, hoping to upset her, was playing tricks with the music. This was also noticed by the Queen, herself an excellent musician, and when Jenny Lind stood up for her second song, the Queen motioned aside the pianist and accompanied the singer herself.

Nos. 133-141 The Great Exhibition of 1851
All these items depict scenes from the Great Exhibition, the idea of which was first mooted by Prince Albert to the Society of Arts in 1849.

The scheme was approved on March 21st 1850, the original proposal being for the exhibition to be held in Somerset House. On investigation, it was realised that the Exhibition as envisaged, would be too large for this suggestion to be effective, the Hyde Park site being chosen as the alternative.

The superintendant of the Duke of Devonshire's estate at Chatsworth, Mr. Joseph Paxton, produced the most original and suitable proposal: a large conservatory type building, 1,848 feet long, 408 feet wide and 66 feet high, enclosing all the trees inside the building to avoid unnecessary tree felling.

The firm decision to build was taken on July 26th 1850, contracts were placed on July 30th, building was commenced on September 26th and completed for painting and fitting by December 31st 1850.

A popular story alleged that Queen Victoria expressed her concern about the large quantity of sparrows which were captives in the large building, and the problems of removing them. The Duke of Wellington solved this problem quite simply, by replying 'Sparrow-hawks, Ma'am, Sparrow-hawks'.

All was completed for the official opening by the Queen on May 1st 1851; approximately 6-7 million people visited the Exhibition, which closed on October 15th 1851 making a profit of £200,000.

These monies were used for the purchase of lands in South Kensington, to be used for the purpose of erecting and maintaining various Exhibition buildings, known today as Exhibition Road. The building was dismantled in 1852 and re-erected at Sydenham, South London. This took two years; it was reopened in 1854 where it was known as the Crystal Palace. It was burned down in 1936.

No. 153 The Late Prince Consort

Prince Albert was taken ill in early December 1861, typhoid fever developed, and, in spite of all attention possible, he died at midnight on Saturday December 14th 1861.

No. 176 Buckingham Palace

Previously known as Buckingham House, this palace was altered and enlarged by John Nash in the reigns of George IV and William IV.

Further alterations were made in 1837 for Queen Victoria. The east front was added in 1850 and at the same time the Marble Arch was removed from the front of the palace and erected on its present site at the north-east corner of Hyde Park.

Nos. 190 and 191 Albert Memorial

This monument was designed by Sir Gilbert Scott R.A. as a memorial to the Prince Consort. The memorial, built in the Victorian Gothic style, composed of marble, gold, bronze and mosaic, and situated in Hyde Park near the site of the 1851 Exhibition, is 175 feet high and was officially opened in 1872. The cost was in excess of £130,000.

No. 214 The Volunteers

In 1859 the movement now known as the Territorials was formed, in response to a growing feeling of distrust with the formation of a considerable armada of ships and men building up in Cherbourg. It was thought that an invasion was imminent. This volunteer movement may have had the desired effect on Napoleon III, because, on seeing these preparations, no invasion took place. The success of this operation decided the government to keep and maintain 'The Volunteers'.

Title	Ref. No.	Page No.
Administrative Building, World's Fair, Chicago 1893	146	95
Alas! Poor Bruin *see* Bear Subjects		
Albert Edward, Prince of Wales, and Princess Alexandra	155	99
Albert Edward, Prince of Wales, and Princess Alexandra of Denmark	128	77
Albert Edward, Prince of Wales, and Princess Alexandra on their Marriage in 1863	157	100
Albert Memorial	190, 191	118
Alexandra Palace 1873	85	59
	200	122
All but Trapped *see* Bear Subjects		
Allied Generals	168	108
Alma	165	106
Arctic Expedition in Search of Sir John Franklin	17	23
Attacking Bears *see* Bear Subjects		
Autumn	342	207
Bacchanalians at Play	379	231
Balaklava, Inkerman, Alma	166	107
Battle of the Alma	75	55
Battle of the Alma (20th September 1854)	74	55
Battle of the Nile, The	210	127
Bay of Naples	124	76
Bear Subjects		
Alas! Poor Bruin	1	17
All but Trapped	20	25
Attacking Bears, The	8	20
Bear Attacked by Dogs	2	18
Bear Hunting	4	19
Bear in a Ravine	14	22
Bear in Cave	21	25
Bear, Lion and Cock	19	24
Bear Pit, The	6	20
Bear with Valentines	11	21
Bears at School	9	21
Bear's Grease Manufacturer	3	18
Bears on Rock	10	21
Bears Reading Newspapers	7	20
Performing Bear, The	12	22
Polar Bears	18	24
Prowling Bear, The	5	19
Shooting Bears	13	22
Two Bears, The	458	285
Bee-hive, The	130	77
Begging Dog, The	270	165
Belle Vue Tavern *see* Pegwell Bay Subjects		
Best Card, The	254	152

Title	Ref. No.	Page No.
Bird Subjects		
Birds	449	282
Blue Tit, The	303	182
Blue Tit and Long-tailed Tit	282	172
Bullfinch, The	298	181
Bullfinch and the Canary	284	173
Buzzard, The	288	174
Chaffinch, The	294	178
Condor, The, and the Snake	290	175
Cuckoo, The	281	172
Eagle Owl and Merlin	292	176
Goldfinch, The	280	171
	301	182
Heron, The	175	291
Kestrel, The	287	174
Kingfisher, The	296	179
Lesser-spotted Woodpecker	306	183
Nightingale, The	295A	178
	300	181
Owl, The	307	183
Red-backed Shrike	305	182, 183
Reed Warbler, The	285	173
Robin, The	278	171
Sea Eagle, The	289	175
Skylark, The	295B	178
Snowy Owl and Young	286	174
Storm Petrel, The	304	183
Swallow, The	267	180
	283	173
Thrush, The	293	176
Wren, The	302	182
Wrens, A Pair of	279	171
Yellow Hammer	299	181
Blackfriars Bridge, The New	196	120
Blind Fiddler, The	417	261
Blind Man's Buff	246	146
Blue Boy, The	174	111, 112
Blue Tit *see* Bird Subjects		
Blue Tit and Long-tailed Tit *see* Bird Subjects		
Boar Hunt, The	262	157
Both Alike	272	167
Bouquet	439	275
Breakfast Party	314	188
Bride, The	97	66
Bridge across the Gap	409	254
Buckingham Palace	176	113
Buffalo Hunt, The	243	145
Bull-fight, The	244	145
Bullfinch *see* Bird Subjects		
Bullfinch and the Canary *see* Bird Subjects		
Bully, The	415	259
Bunch of Cherries	126	76
Buzzard *see* Bird Subjects		

Title	Ref. No.	Page No.
Cattle and Ruins	315	189
Cattle Drover, The	382	235
Cavalier, The	356	219
Cavalier, The, and the Serving Woman	381	234
Chaffinch *see* Bird Subjects		
Charge of the Scots Greys at Balaklava	76	55
Charing Cross	193	119
Chalees Satoon, The	83	58
Chapel Royal	198	121
Charity	362	223
Chatsworth	437	274
Chiefs return from Deer-stalking	248	147
Children of Flora	237	140
Children Sailing Boats in Tub	263	157
Chin-Chew River	218	130
Chinese River Scene with Junks	440	276
Choir of Chapel Royal, Savoy	199	121
Christ in the Cornfield	424	267
Circassian, The	127	77
Condor and the Snake *see* Bird Subjects		
Constantinople — The Golden Horn	80	57
Continental Fish Market	71	53
Continental Scene	383	235
Contrast	266	163
Conway Castle	217	130
Cottage Children	313	188
	313	285
Country Quarters	273	167
Cows in Stream near Ruins	388	234
Crooked Bridge, The	378	230
Crosse and Blackwell's Advertising Plaque	442	277
Crosse and Blackwell Plaque	457	285
Crystal Palace, The	137	92
Crystal Palace (Interior)	139	93
Crystal Palace, Interior View of	138	93
Cuckoo *see* Bird Subjects		
Dangerous Skating	249	148
Deer Drinking	321	194
Deerhound Guarding Cradle	269	164
Deer-stalker, The	92	61
	384	236
Dentist, The	323	195
Derby Day, *see* Race, A		
Dogs	264	158-161
Donkey's Foal, The	386	236
Dragoon Charge — Balaklava, The	77	56
Drayton Manor	179	114
Driving Cattle	387	237
Dublin Industrial Exhibition 1853	143	94
Dutch Fisherman, The	34	31
Dutch River Scene	66	50
Dutch Winter Scene	308	184
Eagle Owl and Merlin *see* Bird Subjects		
Eastern Lady and Black Attendant	100	67
Eastern Lady Dressing Hair	99	66
Eastern Repast, An	98	66
Ecclesiastical Subjects	448	281
Eleanor Cross	194	119
Embarking for the East	206	126
England's Pride	149	97
Enthusiast, The	245	146
Eugenie	456	284
Examining the Nets	54	45
Exhibition Buildings 1851 *see* Great Exhibition Subjects		
Exposition Universelle, L', de 1867	145	95
Exterior View, 1851 Exhibition *see* Great Exhibition Subjects		
Fair Sportswoman	250	148
Faithful Shepherd, The	309	185
Fall of Sebastopol (8th September 1855)	78	56
False Move, A	251	149
Farriers, The	324	197
Feeding the Chickens	267	163
Ferry Boat, The	389	239
Field Marshall the Duke of Wellington *see* Wellington, Duke of		
First Appeal, The	329	199
Fishbarrow	58	47
Fisher-boy, The	341	206
Fisherman's Abode	369	228
Fisherwomen Returning Home	59	48
Fishmarket, The	57	47
Fix, A	256	153
Fleet at Anchor, The	72	54
Floral Subjects	131/1-131/36	78-87
Flute Player, The	337	203
Fording the Stream	335	202
Foreign River Scene	62	49
French Street Scene	312	187
Fruit and Statue Piece	113	72
Fruit, Glass and Wine Decanter	429	271
Funeral of the Late Duke of Wellington *see* Wellington, Duke of		
Game Bag, The	260	155
Garden Terrace, The	115	73
Garibaldi	169	109
Gay Dog, A	268	163
Girl with Grapes	345	209
Golden Horn, Constantinople	204	125
Goldfinch *see* Bird Subjects		
Good Catch, A	459	285
Good Dog	265	162
Gothic Archway	125	76
Grace before Meals	338	204
Grand International Buildings of 1851 *see* Great Exhibition Subjects		
Grapes, Hazelnuts and Medlar	451	283
Great Exhibition Subjects		
Exhibition Buildings 1851	134	91
Exterior View, 1851 Exhibition	96D	65
Grand Exhibition 1851	135	92
Grand International Buildings of 1851	133	90

Title	Ref. No.	Page No.
Great Exhibition 1851	96B	64
Great Exhibition of 1851 (Closing Ceremony)	141	94
Great Exhibition of 1851 (Opening Ceremony)	140	94
Interior of the Grand International Building of 1851	136	92
Grecian Landscape	433	273
Haddon Hall	435	274
Hafod	436	274
Halt by the Wayside	350	214
Halt near Ruins	390	239
Harbour, The, Margate	40	34
Harbour of Hong-Kong	221	132
Hathaway, Ann Hathaway's Cottage	228	135
Hauling in the Trawl	53	45
Heron see Bird Subjects		
Hide and Seek	255	152
High Life	274	168
Highland Music	418	262
Holborn Viaduct	202	123
Holy Trinity Church, Stratford-on-Avon	136	229
Hop Queen, The	414	258
Horse Drawing Boat to Land	403	248
Houses of Parliament, New	195	119
Houses of Parliament, New, Westminster	183	116
Houses of Parliament, The	184	116
How I Love to Laugh	367	227
Huntley and Palmer's Plaque	455	284
I See You My Boy	311	187
Independence Hall, Philadelphia, Interior View	444A	278
Injury	50	40
Ins, The	15	23
Interior of the Grand International Building of 1851 see Great Exhibition Subjects		
International Exhibition 1862	144	95
Irishman, The	357B	220
Jewsbury & Brown Plate	454	284
Johnson, Dr.	175	112
Jolly Topers	406	252
Jones, Sir Harry	79	56
Kestrel see Bird Subjects		
Kingfisher see Bird Subjects		
Lady, Boy and Goats	316	190
Lady, Boy and Mandoline	109	71
Lady Brushing Hair	111	71
Lady Fastening Shoe	110	71
Lady Reading Book	105	68
Lady with Guitar	107	70
Lady with Hawk	106	70
Landing of the British Army at the Crimea	73	54
Landing the Catch see Pegwell Bay Subjects		
Landing the Fare see Pegwell Bay Subjects		
Landscape and River Scene	416	260
Last In, The	412	256
Late Duke of Wellington see Wellington, Duke of		
Lend a Bite	317	191
Lesser-spotted Woodpecker see Bird Subjects		
Letter from the Diggings	360	222
Lind, Jenny	116	73
Listener, The	363	224
Little Red-riding Hood	358	220
Lovers, The	119	74
Low Life	275	168
Maidens Decorating Bust of Homer	380a	233
Maidservant, The	343	208
Master of the Hounds	247	147
Matador, The	114	72
May Day Dancers at the Swan Inn	233	138
Medieval Mansion	374	229
Meditation	122	75
Meet of the Foxhounds	81	57
Meeting of Garibaldi and Victor Emmanuel	211	128
Mending the Nets	56	46
	70	53
Milking the Cow	86	59
	391	240
Milkmaid, The	443	277
Mirror, The	101	67
Monastery in Alton Towers	427	270
Monastic Ruins	371	228
Mother and Daughters	320	194
Mountain Stream	423	266
Music Lesson, The	380	233
Musical Trio	123	75
Napier, Admiral Sir Charles, C.B.	167	108
Napirima, Trinidad	225	133
Napirima, Trinidad (with advertising)	225A	133
Napoleon III and Empress Eugenie	156	99
Negro and Pitcher	344	208
Nelson Crescent, Ramsgate	43	36
Net-mender, The	60	48
New Jetty and Pier, Margate	39	34
New York Exhibition, 1853	142	94
Nightingale see Bird Subjects		
Ning Po River	222	132
Old Jack	215	129
Old Water-mill, The	318	192
On Guard	340	205
Ornamental Garden, The	121	75
Osborne House	182	115
Our Home	241	144
Our Pets	242	144
Outs, The	16	23
Owl see Bird Subjects		
Packman, The	103	68
Pair, A	252	150

Title	Ref. No.	Page No.
Paris Exhibition 1878	148	96
Parish Beadle, The	236	139
Passing the Pipe	90	60
	404	250
Peabody	171	110
Peace	220	131
Peace (after Wouvermann)	213	128
Peasant Boys	348	211
Pegwell Bay Subjects		
Belle Vue — Pegwell Bay	30	29
Belle Vue Tavern	29	28
Belle Vue Tavern (with carriage)	28	29
Belle Vue Tavern (with cart)	27	28
Landing the Catch	55	46
Landing the Fare — Pegwell Bay	38	34
Pegwell Bay	23	26
Pegwell Bay and Cliffs	67, 68	51
Pegwell Bay, Banger, S., Shrimp Sauce Manufacturer	32	30
Pegwell Bay. Established 1760	25	27
Pegwell Bay — Four Shrimpers	26	27
Pegwell Bay — Kent	69	53
Pegwell Bay (Lobster Fishing)	24	26
Pegwell Bay, Ramsgate (Farmyard Scene)	37	32
Pegwell Bay, Ramsgate (Still-life Fish)	36	32
Pegwell Bay, Ramsgate (Still-life Game)	35	32
Pegwell Bay Shrimpers	31	29
Pegwell Bay (Shrimping)	33	30
Penseroso, Il	235	139
Performing Bear *see* Bear Subjects		
Persuasion	353	217
Pet Rabbits	234	138
Pheasant Shooting	261	156
Philadelphia Exhibition 1876	147	96
	444C	278
Philadelphia Public Building 1876	444	278
Picnic, The	354	218
Polar Bears *see* Bear Subjects		
Pompey and Caesar	271	166
Poultry Woman, The	349	212
Poultry Yard, The, Trentham	425	269
Pratt, Felix Edwards	173	111
Preparing for the Ride	351	215
Pretty Kettle of Fish	48	38
Prince Albert (Hare Coursing) *see* Windsor Castle		
Prince Consort, The Late	153	99
Prince of Wales, H.R.H., visiting the Tomb of Washington	310	185
Prowling Bear *see* Bear Subjects		
Quarry, The	352	216
Queen, The, God Bless Her	319	193
Race, A, *or* Derby Day	257	154
Reception of H.R.H. The Prince of Wales and Princess Alexandra at London Bridge, 7th March 1863	96	63
Red Bull Inn, The	359	221
Red-backed Shrike *see* Bird Subjects		
Redoubt, The	216	129
Reed Warbler *see* Bird Subjects		
Reflection in Mirror	104	68
Revenge	51	40
Rhine Scene, A	408	254
Rifle Contest, Wimbledon 1864	224	133
Rivals, The	322	195
River Scene with Boat (R.W.)	61	48
Robin *see* Bird Subjects		
Roman Ruins	420	264
Roman Ruins and Pedestrians	441	276
Rose Garden, The	120	74
Round Tower, The	370	228
Rowland's Kalydor	453	382
Rowland's Odonto	452	283
Royal Arms and Allied Flags of the Crimea	129	77
Royal Children — Windsor Castle	447	280
Royal Coat of Arms	95A	62
	355	218
Royal Coat of Arms (J. Gosnell & Co.)	450	282
Royal Exchange	95	62
Royal Harbour, Ramsgate	41, 42	35
Ruined Abbey Chancel	376	229
Ruined Temples	373	228
Ruined Tower	377a	229
Rural Scene, A	428	270
Rustic Laundrywoman, The	422	265
St. Paul's Cathedral	94	62
	192	118
	192A	119
St. Paul's Cathedral and River Pageant	185	116
St. Thomas's Hospital, New	203	123
Sandown Castle, Kent	44	36
Sandringham	181	115
Sea Eagle *see* Bird Subjects		
Sea Nymph with Trident	64	50
Sea-shore Study, A	96A	63
	393	241
Second Appeal, The	330	200
Sebastopol	208	126
	208A, 209	127
Shakespeare's Birthplace (Exterior)	226	134
Shakespeare's Birthplace (Interior)	227	135
Shells	52A-52L	41-44
Shooting Bears *see* Bear Subjects		
Shrimpers, The	63	49
Shrine, The	372	228
Skaters, The	258	154
Skewbald Horse, The	277	170
Skylark *see* Bird Subjects		
Smokers, The	93	62
	405	251
Snap-dragon	253	151
Snow-drift	276	169
Snowy Owl and Young *see* Bird Subjects		
Soyer's Advertising Plaque	446	279
Spanish Dancers, The	431	272
Spanish Lady, The	112	72
Sportsman, The	259	154
Spring	342	207

Title	Ref. No.	Page No.
Stall-woman, The	445	279
State House in Philadelphia 1776	444B	278
Stone Bridge, The	394	241
Stone Jetty, The	89	60
	395	242
Storm Petrel *see* Bird Subjects		
Strasburg	331	200
Strathfieldsay	187	117
Strathfieldsaye	188	117
Strawberry Girl, The	364	225
Street Scene on the Continent	336	203
Stowe, Harriet Beecher	172	110
Summer	342a	207
Swallow *see* Bird Subjects		
Swing, The	239	142
Swiss Riverside Scene	65	50
Tam-o-Shanter	347	210
Tam-o-Shanter and Souter Johnny	346	210
Thames Embankment	197	120
Thirsty Soldier, The	205	125
Thrush *see* Bird Subjects		
Times, The	327	198
Toilette, The	102	67
Toll Bridge, The	375	229
Torrent, The	88	60
	411	255
Tower of London, The	186	117
Trafalgar Square	201	122
Transplanting Rice	332	201
Traveller's Departure, The	82	57
	396	243
Travelling Knife-grinder, The	419	263
Tremadoc	430	271
Trentham Hall	426	269, 270
Tria Juncta in Uno	164	104
Trooper, The	334	202
Truant, The	413	257
Tryst, The	117	73
Trysting Place, The	118	74
Two Anglers, The	432	272
Two Bears *see* Bear Subjects		
Tyrolese Hill Scene	410	255
Tyrolese Village Scene	87	59
	397	244
Uncle Toby	328	198
Uncle Tom	402	247
Uncle Tom and Eva	91	61
	401	247
Unwelcome Attentions	438	274

Title	Ref. No.	Page No.
Venice	84	58
Victoria, Queen, and Albert Edward	154	99
Victoria, Queen, and the Prince Consort	152	98
Victoria, Queen, on Balcony	150	97
Victoria, Queen, with Orb and Sceptre	151	98
View near St. Michael's Mount	407	253
Village Scene on the Continent	398	244
Village Wakes, The	232	137
Village Wedding, The	240	143
Vine Girl, The	339	205
Volunteers, The	214	129
Vue de la Ville de Strasbourg Prise du Port	333	201
Walmer Castle	45, 47	39
Walmer Castle (with sentry)	46	37
War	219	131
War (after Wouvermann)	212	128
Washington Crossing the Delaware	207	126
Watering Cattle	377	229
Waterfall, The	365	226
Wellington, Duke of		
Field Marshall the Duke of Wellington	162	103
Funeral of the Late Duke of Wellington	163	103
Late Duke of Wellington Obit. September 14th 1852	161	102
Wellington (with clasped hands)	160	101
Wellington with Cocked Hat	158, 159	100
Westminster Abbey	189	118
Wild Deer, The	92A	61
	385	236
Wimbledon, July 1860	223	132
Windmill, The	399	245
Windsor Castle *or* Prince Albert (Hare Coursing)	178	114
Windsor Castle and St. George's Chapel	177	113
Windsor Castle (Hill & Ledger)	96C	64
Windsor Park (Returning from Stag-hunting)	180	115
Wolf and the Lamb, The	361	223
Wooden Bridge, The	400	245, 246
Wooer, The	108	70
Wren *see* Bird Subjects		
Wrens, A Pair of, *see* Bird Subjects		
Xmas Eve	238	140
Yellow Hammer *see* Bird Subjects		
Youth and Age	366	227

PRICES

Collectors are once again reminded that **condition** is the final criterion. Ware is always subject to more usage than lids and is therefore expected to show more signs of wear such as rubbing, loss of colour, chips, scratches, etc. The prices given are for specimens in good condition and due allowance must be made for wear. Some items are marked P.B.N.; this means price by negotiation.